ISBN: 978-1-60920-080-0

Printed in the United States of America
©2013 Astrig Tutelian
Library of Congress Cataloging in Publication Data

API
Ajoyin Publishing, Inc.
P.O. 342
Three Rivers, MI 49093
www.ajoyin.com

Please direct your inquiries to admin@ajoyin.com

My Life's Journey . . .

Astrig Tutelian

Dedicated to my Husband

Contents

Preface

At the threshold of my life's three-quarter-century mark, even though some memories had become slightly hazy, yet, an unseen force urged me to look back at the chain of events that created the tapestry of my life, and compelled me to write them down for no apparent reason. Perhaps it was the need to express my gratitude for the life I was blessed to have been granted that caused me to finally give in, sit down, and casually begin to put down on paper some of the highlights of the past seventy-five years' experiences, which were uniquely mine. My life was and still is an undeserved gift, freely given to me by the grace of God.

So this is an invitation for you to peek into my life's story, with the desire not only to entertain, but to share with you some of my past personal encounters that helped me grow and mature through struggles at every turn and chapter of my life; I consider them to be nothing but tiny miracles. Looking back as far as I can see, it is quite apparent to me that at times the events which shaped my life were securely and neatly woven into colorful, exquisite designs; still others appear loosely braided, hanging frightfully in space with no visible support. Yet all were finally synchronized harmoniously in what is crystal clear now, perhaps not then: that an invisible hand was weaving, protecting, sustaining, nurturing, and directing my life from the very beginning of my self-consciousness.

Chapter One

End of my Teenage Years

Painfully shy with deep-seated complexes and insecurities, I tried desperately as a child to make myself invisible. I had no earthly reason to feel unloved or unwanted, for I was intensely loved just as genuinely as my siblings. Still, in a buried dark and secret corner of my soul where I often hid to suffer privately with tears and in agony, I could hear in my mind an unrelenting and merciless voice tormenting me: *You are short, fat, and ugly . . . No one loves you and no one ever will.*

I was very good at hiding my true feelings, so no one suspected or even had a clue of the depth of my secretly held anguish. To the overly sensitive, musical, and creative child that I was, these destructive thoughts were excruciatingly painful. I simply was too weak to fight against their power over me; what's more, I was too timid to discuss my emotional turmoil with anyone.

I was taught from the cradle that God loved me, and that he would listen and understand our needs; so with the simple faith of a child my prayers often ended with this sincere plea: *Lord, you have chosen not to give me physical beauty; I pray you would create in me a beautiful soul.*

It is ironic and unbelievable that during this awkward period of my life, my loving father, whom I adored intensely, was totally unaware of my secret feelings. Very often Dad would hug me adoringly. With his tender voice and gentle smile he would reaffirm his love for me while proudly announcing, as if to the whole world "You are my beautiful and delicious daughter." He had nicknamed me "Caramella" . . . and who doesn't know how sweet caramels are?

I was told many a time that I was loved by my parents and the family at large. Moreover, that God also loved me with an immeasurable, eternal love. I believed all of this to be true in my head; however, I needed to, but couldn't feel it down deep in my soul. Sadly, when you think so little of yourself and feel unworthy of love, you cannot love yourself, and when given, you cannot receive it. So you become incapable of enjoying the redeeming power of love, be it human or divine.

It is totally illogical that one can be raised in a solidly loving home with caring parents and siblings, be well provided for with all earthly goods and in addition to having all her social, educational, physical, and religious needs met, and yet can bury feelings of being unwanted and unloved in the shadows of her mind. One can only imagine how a real orphan or a truly unwanted child must feel. I had no excuses, none.

Now as an adult looking back into my childhood, I can see no one, absolutely no one, who could be blamed for my negative and disparaging beliefs. Who knows? Perhaps those harmful thoughts and feelings were inborn; but they surely robbed me of a happy, carefree childhood, wasting the brief, precious years of my early youth, depleting my energies, which resulted in my slow and delayed development to healthy maturity.

It is utterly amazing to me that with all the turmoil that was going on in my soul, I, a mere child, at the age of twelve, brought up protected as if in a cocoon with no concept of what life was all about—its pitfalls, dangers, and temptations—felt compelled to heed that still, small voice deep inside me, persistently whispering, till in time it became a clear and strong sense of knowledge. I had a deep conviction that when the time was right, I was to leave Egypt—where I was born and spent my formative years—my family, church community, physical and material comforts, and move thirteen thousand miles away from home to California.

I was born into a musical family; we all sang and played some kind of a musical instrument. I had taken piano lessons since I was six. At fifteen or sixteen years of age, I was the youngest member in our church choir when we presented Handel's *Messiah* in a formal concert with full orchestra the first time ever in Egypt. I was often told that I had a beautiful voice: besides, I simply loved to sing; so naturally that's what I would do when I got to the States: further develop my musical abilities.

Undoubtedly you can well imagine that when I made known to my parents my deep-rooted belief concerning my imminent future, they were convinced that at twelve, this was only a childhood dream or an expression of my dramatized imaginings. I am sure that at first my persistence must have sounded like a joke to my parents, especially to my mother, who could not begin to fathom such a happening and repeatedly dismissed the whole idea. Her reaction was always the same: "You are only a child, where do you think you are going?"

However, a few years later, when at sixteen I was still frequently repeating my mantra, she realized I was not giving up my dream. Then she tried unsuccessfully to discourage me with as much conviction as she could muster. She would caution me by saying, "If you go, I will not support you financially." I always responded to that with the self-confidence of an adult, even though I knew full well that I was not prepared to do any meaningful work to provide for myself. Confidently I would remind her that everyone worked in the United States, and so would I.

My father, on the other hand, had a similar, yet unfulfilled dream of his own as a youth; because of it he was far more sympathetic to my aspirations than my mother. He never voiced an objection, but each time during subsequent years when I would bring up the subject of my future plans, he would only look deep into my eyes and smile knowingly. My father's quiet demeanor was a sign of his understanding and approval; he never contradicted my mother openly, at least not in my presence.

Every time I mentioned with great certainty what I called my imminent future, I assured my mom that I would never leave home without her full consent. Though she was not aware of it or willing as of yet, I knew in my heart that when the time was right, she would willingly give me her wholehearted blessing, without which I solemnly promised never to go away.

After seven whole years with persistent reminders of my inevitable destiny, like a miracle, it happened. With the help of both my parents plus the connection we had with our previous pastor, then in Fresno, just four short months later the Bible institute I was to attend was contacted. Without any difficulty we soon received the required application forms, prepared specifically for foreign students.

Without delay on our part we completed the necessary official papers and took care of all the required medical exams. The mandatory documents were all ready with clocklike precision and were mailed back to Fresno with the speed of a whirlwind. Shortly after, to my indescribable excitement, we received their letter of acceptance; they were happy and looking forward with anticipation to have me attend their college in the fall of the same year. Oh, what joy and relief!

So finally the time had come for me to go and present myself to the American Consul, submit myself to an interview, pick up my finalized papers, and have my student's entry visa to the States stamped in my passport.

Worried that I might say something which could sabotage my case, I was terrified to go alone for this final and crucially important interview. I went downtown Alexandria to see my dad at our family-owned, twin stores, to ask him if he would accompany me for moral support one last time, as he had always done during the preliminary preparations; but to my deep disappointment, he unwaveringly refused to comply.

In his gentle way, he patiently explained that if I could not walk a few blocks down the street alone without him by my side, present myself and be interviewed by the American Consul, pick up my completed official documents and visa for my departure, he would be seriously concerned, wondering if I was indeed ready to leave home to face and handle my future on my own.

It was only later that I realized how loving and wise my father was. This was to be his final and major attempt to teach me, at the twelfth hour, self-reliance, to help build my self-confidence more than his own; so that I would know beyond a shadow of a doubt that I was capable of handling the rest of my life without parental guidance and help. I respected and loved my father all the more for it.

This was truly a test, a time for me to try my wings . . . sink or swim. If I failed, the stakes were exceedingly high, so whispering constant little prayers, still fearful and anxious, I was on my way to find out if my file was prepared and completed properly. Hoping that I was up to the task before me, I started walking toward the American Consulate.

Surprised at my own audacity, and courage, I carried myself with an amazing inner strength I did not know I had. After a successful interview, I got my papers and visa, was warmly congratulated by the Consul General himself, and with my officially stamped passport, walking as if on air, I returned to my father.

Wow, such victory! Indeed it was then, and only then, I knew for sure I was ready and capable of leaving home permanently. Finally . . . America, here I come!

> *Thank you, Lord, for my father's love,*
> *and great wisdom, and for providing me*
> *with the courage I needed.*

Chapter Two

Crossing the Oceans

To this day it is still incredible to me that it all happened like a destiny being fulfilled. I had received a wholehearted blessing from my father and mother before we began preparations for the longest, most adventurous and daring journey of my life, that is literally and figuratively. I wonder if, as a parent, I would have had the courage to do the same.

After making the rounds of formal good-byes to family and friends in Alexandria, my parents and I took the train for Cairo to spend a couple of days with other extended family members, to see and bid them farewell before my departure. Among them was my very loving fraternal grandmother, Mariam. Grandma was old and ailing; I knew in my heart that this was to be the last time I would see and hug her. My heart was breaking;

she was the most difficult person to say good-bye to.

In a day or two we left for Port Said for an overnight stay; from there I was to get on board the ship that was to take me away from my family and home. The hour was nearer than ever before when I had to cut the umbilical cord and take my final, perhaps permanent, leave from my parents.

My itinerary and the means of travel were paid in full and arranged all the way to California by my father. To spare me from possible difficulties at different European ports, he had wisely chosen a nonstop passage to the States. The ship I was to take was in her maiden voyage. She was to come from the South Seas into the Suez Canal, then at a snail's pace move on and enter into the vicinity of Port Said Harbor. Still moving constantly, she was to pick up one young passenger before entering the open waters of the Mediterranean.

Midmorning of that unforgettable day, my parents and I were taken in a small steamboat to what seemed quite a distance from the shoreline into the harbor waters; we were rocking continuously with the moderate movements of the gentle waves. As if crawling with extreme caution, we had come uncomfortably close to and were moving parallel alongside this brand new, beautiful cargo liner. The men who were in control of our steamboat were extraordinarily careful while keeping pace with the midsize ship that was to take me away from everything I knew and was comfortably familiar with.

They lowered a long staircase from the boat. There was no time for long good-byes or tears, and so, after quick, heartfelt hugs, still swaying to and fro in that tiny boat, I uneasily climbed that insecure-looking, midair hanging stairs. Later, standing at a handrail, fearful that they might accidently drop one of my suitcases into the sea, I watched the luggage carriers bring them all up safely into the advancing vessel. I was the only passenger that boarded the ship at Port Said, and was also to be the last till we reached America on this fifteen-day, continuous journey.

Immediately after they raised the stairway, the porters, having returned to the steamboat, turned the small vessel around as fast as they could and headed toward the harbor in full speed, taking my parents with them. At the same time the boat I was on gradually but definitely began to pick up pace, going steadily farther and farther from the harbor into the open waters of the Mediterranean Sea.

Tirelessly we kept on waving good-bye while slowly but surely being navigated apart from each other. This was the inevitable point of no return; the deep feeling of profound loneliness in my soul was overwhelming.

I stood there motionless at the railing with misty eyes and an intense ache in my heart; I saw the figures of my loved ones getting smaller and smaller as they were moving closer and closer to the harbor. I kept staring at them for as long as I could with an acute love and deep gratitude in my heart for all that they had sacrificed for me to date, the greatest of which was at that very moment in time, when they let me go to pursue what seemed to me to be my sacredly held dream. I kept my eyes glued on them with blurred vision, without blinking, till I finally lost sight of them.

It had been biblically the complete and total number of seven years since I had told my parents of my inevitable future. It was just two weeks after my nineteenth birthday that I found myself on this immaculately clean, first-class Norwegian cargo liner. I was given a deluxe suite with private accommodations, as were each of the other nine passengers on board.

We were all to be traveling together as a family for the next two weeks, sailing ten thousand miles westward, heading toward the East Coast of the United States. The next leg of my journey was to be on land; in three days and nights, I was to cross this vast country on two separate trains for another three thousand miles, going still farther west to reach my final destination: beautiful, sunny California.

Incredibly, I felt no apprehension, but was bursting with anticipation and overflowing eagerness to begin my new life. My heart was almost exploding with excitement even though this boat was carrying me away from home; yet at the same time, moment by moment it was bringing me closer and closer to my destiny. Though I was already missing my family, yet I felt no fear of the unknown loneliness ahead, nor had the slightest sense of anxiety for the lack of personal and monetary security I had just left behind. I was somewhat stress-free with the knowledge that the school I was to attend was providing me with a full scholarship, a dormitory room, and part living expenses.

Even though my parents had requested permission from the government to assist me financially on a regular basis while I was studying abroad, the law at the time did not allow it. Except for the officially allocated mere sixty dollars in my pocket, I was not permitted to further receive any monetary support from home. With no travel or medical insurance, I was on my way, ready to face my future. With today's standards, that is mind-boggling. Unbelievable!

Having had parents who were sincere believers, I, from a very young age—practically from the cradle—was reared with biblical precepts. I believed that God loved me, and knew in my heart that he would not leave nor forsake me. He was the One who had instigated and set this path before me, kept the conviction alive in my heart for so many years, and literally facilitated miraculously the completion of my official papers for my departure, just in the nick of time.

Only five months after I left Egypt in 1956, a war broke out in the Middle East over the Suez Canal, which would have made my departure literally impossible. That would have changed the sum of my life story and the experiences that shaped my life to this day.

Brought up conservatively and extremely protected, I had not ventured nor was encouraged to go to downtown Alexandria unaccompanied, only a distance of a few short miles; and yet now, still a teenager, on board this ship alone, traveling thousands of miles away from home, I felt safe, happy, and excited without any sense of apprehension. It must be true when they say there is bliss in ignorance. I was moving far away from home with no plans or intent of returning, neither had any hope of ever reuniting with my family here, on this side of the Atlantic.

Many have called this, my bold undertaking, brave; but I didn't feel courageous, heroic, or even clever enough to make my life choices and decisions wisely. I only knew I had to follow faithfully that inner, persistent voice. Like a child I simply trusted and relied on God's promises, his loving care, strength, wisdom, and direction. No regrets, no not one.

I soon found out that all passengers on cargo lines have their meals elegantly served at the officers' and captain's table. Tired physically, drained emotionally, slightly nauseous, and naturally feeling homesick as well, I had no appetite neither felt any hunger, so I missed the first evening's dinner.

The next morning when our captain, an elderly, caring, grandfatherlike man, did not see me at the breakfast table as well, he knew by instinct that I might have a touch of homesickness and was not suffering from serious seasickness; so right after his morning coffee, he came, knocked on the door, and entered my stateroom. This compassionate man wanted me to clearly understand that he would personally come and drag me out of bed if I skipped another meal. You can be sure I was at the captain's table at lunch the very same day.

Being the youngest passenger on board, not only the captain but my fellow travelers as well were aware of the fact that I was away from home for the first time ever, so they were all very sensitive and gentle with me. Among my traveling companions was an elderly, endearing, American couple who were returning home from their six-month-long, round-the-world trip—a soft-spoken, retired air force colonel and his petite, pretty wife.

She became and remained my guardian angel throughout our long journey while we crossed the vast, deep, and endless waters. It was as if from day one God was reassuring me that I was not alone. We used to have long talks about my dreams and future aspirations; she was preparing me for my upcoming life in America. She had a soft spot in her heart for me and I knew it; I too became quite fond of her as well and genuinely, deeply appreciated her sincere friendship.

Lord, thank you for providing, even for a short while, a new, trustworthy friend.

Chapter Three

First Boston, Then Staten Island

A stonishingly none of us became bored during the long two week, non stop travel on water. Unlike cruise lines of today which offer all kinds of entertainment, we amused ourselves by singing familiar songs to one of our fellow traveler's accordion accompaniment; some played cards, backgammon, or chess. There was a diversity of interesting people on this journey. We got to know each other by sharing our life stories, and enjoyed having interesting conversations on a variety of subjects.

After Port Said, besides a narrow strip of earth at the crossing of the Straits of Gibraltar, we did not see any dry land. We had sailed westward the length of the Mediterranean Sea and the whole width of the Atlantic Ocean for two full weeks; then finally, very early one morning, there it was . . . land again!

We had been told there were two changes in our itinerary; our first stop was to be Boston, and next Staten Island instead of New York as was originally scheduled. Apparently cargo lines do this often as demands are wired in for last-minute pickup and delivery of merchandise.

With wide-open eyes, I was drinking in all the sights and sounds as we approached the harbor. This was to be my very first impression of America. Finally, we docked at Boston Harbor, where we were all interviewed and had our documents thoroughly checked by immigration personnel who had come on board to verify the authenticity of our papers. Before it was my turn to meet the officers, the colonel and his wife were interviewed and had their papers approved in no time.

My sweet, newfound friend was well aware of my apprehension and concern over the accuracy or completeness of my file. Perhaps it was illogical, but I was quite fearful that one unforeseen deficiency could by law force them to send me all the way back to Egypt that very same day, with that very same boat. I was immensely grateful when I found out that my guardian angel had demanded and gotten their consent to sit by me for moral support during their questioning and review of my documents.

There were three immigration personnel seated behind a large desk in the interrogating room. The highest-ranking officer, who unquestionably was aware of my anxiety, after glancing through a couple of pages in my file, amused at his own discovery, succeeded to put me at ease without delay by saying that naturally, a student coming to attend a Bible school could not be a criminal.

I, totally unaware and ignorant of the politics of the time, was quite surprised when in jest the same officer asked me if I was a Communist or if I ever was a member of the Communist party. Everyone present in that room knew that my being a Communist was highly unlikely, so they all chuckled as if sharing a joke. This thoughtful government representative had indirectly succeeded to further relax me, at least for the moment.

After that he went through the rest of my official papers in detail; to me that seemed an eternity. Finally he looked up to inform me that everything was in order; however, one very important paper was missing in my files. I could definitely feel, actually hear my heart pounding, racing with panic, and dropping into my extremely nervous stomach with a thud. Instantly I froze with fear.

Immediately, to my deepest appreciation and relief, this sweet angel of mine came to the rescue. She asked if a copy of that particular form was available; and if so, she would like to have a copy of it. Looking at the document supplied to her in just a few seconds, she asked for a pen, completed the questionnaire, and signed it. I was not aware at the time, but with that, she had agreed to become my personal guarantor right then and there. Voilà, literally, in a moment, my file was made complete. Here was a total stranger whom I had met only a couple of weeks before; officially, in a few seconds she had become my very own special sponsor. By divine grace, she was there to rescue and save me from imminent trouble.

Lord, indeed you work in mysterious ways.

The main interrogator and I shook hands warmly like old friends. With great excitement and enthusiasm I informed him that I was invited to go sightseeing with my newfound friends, and asked if I needed my passport or another document as proof of my identity before disembarking.

The officer could not have missed the obvious animation in my voice and the anticipation on my face. That's when he really looked at me for the first time with a big, genuine smile and with true pride in his voice, he said, "My dear, you have come to a free country; now you are free too. Go and enjoy your day; no need to take any papers with you." Those heartfelt words I shall never forget!"

With a lump in my throat—which still happens to me every time I relive that moment—I thanked the kind gentleman and then quickly joined my friends for our daylong excursion into Boston. Off the boat, my very first step on the land of my dreams was indescribably emotional. It is no mystery to me that new immigrants often are moved to kiss the ground when they first come into this country.

> *Lord, here I am in America at last!*
> *Thank you for having brought me safely*
> *thus far.*

The three of us—the gentle colonel, my angel, and I— took a long, leisurely horse-and-buggy ride through the streets of Boston like regular tourists. Later we walked several blocks through the city, with me excitedly almost always running a few steps ahead of them. I could hardly contain myself. They must have gotten a big kick out of watching me as I looked like a little child at a country fair or a candy store for the very first time.

You can imagine their bewilderment when, going down a narrow street, I stopped abruptly, awestruck, and asked them to stand still for a minute. Once more I looked at what I had just seen ahead at the end of the street, this time intently for a longer time; I recognized the wrought iron railing and remembered well the famous park beyond its fence. I knew I had seen it all in a home movie only a few short years before. Then I said to them with great certainty: "Now, when we get to the end of this street, turn and look to your far right. At that end of the park, just outside the fence, you will see an old, red brick church with a tall, white steeple. Just below the steeple there will be a small balcony. This place of worship is called the 'Church in the Park,' and I believe to this day they preach the Gospel every Sunday morning from that balcony for the people in the street and for those who are gathered in the park."

Somewhat puzzled and confused, they did just as I suggested, and when they saw the church as I had described in such detail, they looked at me with utmost bewilderment as if I were extraordinarily clairvoyant. Seeing their expressions, I was amused, but promptly assured them that I was not a psychic, and to their delight quickly clarified the mystery.

That was a wonderfully memorable, exhilarating first day in America. I enjoyed the sounds and the sights, the hustle and the bustle, the aliveness of the city, and most of all I enjoyed sharing it with my new-found friends. But too soon my initial and most thrilling day in America had to come to an end.

I was feeling sad as we headed back to the boat, for that was to be our last evening meal together; later the same night, we would be sailing to our final destination, Staten Island. There I knew we had to say our permanent good-byes, my special angel friend and the colonel, her kind and generous husband. It was not going to be easy to say Godspeed to all the rest of the passengers as well; we had firmly bonded during the past two weeks.

The next and final morning, I went up quite early to see all that I could as we approached the island. Remembering the history and the incredible stories of emigrants past, indescribable feelings went through my whole being as I got my first glimpse of the Statue of Liberty. In a short while we came closer and closer to this magnificent figure, which has become the symbol of deliverance for many, I was glad I was all alone with no one else standing there beside me on the deck.

This was a very emotional, private moment; many times I had seen pictures of this unforgettable lady, and yet this time it was so very different; she was actually, literally standing there with her torch in plain view. Now, she was also the emblem of *my* freedom, *my* hopes, and the realization of *my* dreams. I could feel my throat tightening as I attempted to hold my tears back; I tried but could not take a deep breath. Tears were running down my cheeks. This grand lady was indescribably beautiful. Every one of my mixed feelings that were carefully and deeply hidden in my soul for so long surfaced with great intensity; it was as if I was having an out-of-body experience. I felt I had finally come home; this factual reaction is incomprehensible and inexplicable to those who are born in this blessed land.

Staten Island was the last-minute change of port for our disembarkation. The captain, who was regularly keeping a parental watch over me, had contacted my mother's cousin in New Jersey before our arrival, making sure that he would come to Staten Island to meet me instead of New York Harbor as previously arranged. My heart was full of gratitude, for it seemed by providence someone was always there to help me at every step of my two-week journey.

When we docked, my cousin was already there to welcome me. I had never met him or his family before. He kindly took me to their home for a few days where I met his immediate and extended family. His sister invited me to come for a delicious, home-cooked meal, reminiscent of my mother's. His younger brother, who knew and was quite fond of my mom, drove from Connecticut just to meet me; he was a pianist and a composer, a soft-spoken, gracious man who spent the day driving me around to show me the sights of New Jersey and Manhattan's skyline from across the Hudson River. He was warm and generous to me with his time.

In New Jersey, in their home neighborhood, I was introduced to my first supermarket; this was something quite new to me, different from the small, individually owned grocery stores I was familiar with. I had heard of and knew of televisions, so it was exciting to see my very first one, still in its black-and-white infancy. Some were as small as four inches by four inches built into a large piece of furniture.

My cousin's daughter—my contemporary, a very sweet girl—and I spent a whole day in the most exciting city, the "Big Apple." In New York we had lunch from coin-operated machines like typical New Yorkers; sandwiches and soft drinks cost mere pennies in those days. Automated shopping was unheard of in

Egypt, so some things were totally different and new; yet others, quite the same and familiar.

Although I was raised in two large and crowded cosmopolitan cities, it amazed me to see millions of people just on Broadway alone, countless people hurrying to and fro. The auto traffic, the noise, the heat, and the dirty pavement all reminded me of the streets in Cairo; I thought to myself, "Boy! I am glad I am on my way to California. If they paid me, I would not want to live in New York City."

Many years later I had my chance to work and live in Manhattan. Yes! You guessed it correctly: without a second thought, I welcomed the unique opportunity with open arms. Soon my few days in New Jersey came to an end; I thanked them all for their kind hospitality and was ready to continue my journey.

I have to move on now, Father; please stay with me.

Chapter Four

Crystal Lake on the Way to California

I was more than pleased when Mom's cousin offered to drive me to New York Central Station for the continuation of my journey. He personally helped check in my larger suitcases directly to Fresno, and made sure I boarded in the correct train on time. I thanked him again for their kind hospitality, particularly for his personal help; I wished him and his family well, and got on the train with the rest of my belongings to continue my travel westward as planned.

Midmorning the next day, we arrived Chicago where I had to change trains from New York Central to Santa Fe, in which I was to continue my journey for two more days and nights, till we reached California. I was happy to find out that I had plenty of time to change platforms, and that my next scheduled departure was a couple of hours away. There I remembered promising my father that when I got to Chicago, I would call his longtime, close friend Theodore, who with his family had left for Crystal Lake many years earlier.

I noticed a booth with what looked like a telephone in it. I was quite familiar with our direct-dial, home telephone, but just like the younger generation of today, I had never seen or used an operator-assisted pay phone before. As soon as I went into the booth to make my call, a woman came and stood outside the door to wait for her turn.

I had no idea how much each call cost, or that I had to make a long-distance connection for the phone number I had. I innocently began dialing; then to my great astonishment, a voice in the receiver said, "Hello, what number are you trying to call please?"

Boy! Never had I been so glad to have finished the British high school back home and was able to communicate with the operator; besides, luckily I was familiar with American currency. She told me I needed to put the exact change into the plainly marked slots, without which I could not make my call.

I was grateful for the information I got from her, and then begged her to stay on the line till I could go back to the ticket window and get the necessary coins. I made my way running through the crowd, stood in line waiting for my turn, finally got the correct change, and hurried back. That took a little while; when I came back, that poor woman was still standing there waiting impatiently to make her call. For her I was not fast enough, and she clearly looked annoyed with me.

But that was only step one; I still had to overcome my next hurdle, which was to find out how to put in the coins! The operator told me the correct amount I needed, and that I should put the exact sum in their proper slots. She was quite patient with me; clearly my foreign accent and obvious ignorance was a strong clue that I was a newcomer to this country. I took the first quarter and unsuccessfully pushed it in its well-marked space; again and again I pushed, and kept pushing it in even harder and still harder, but with no results.

With all my belongings, which included a winter coat, overheated and squeezed in that small telephone booth, I was well aware and concerned for the lady waiting just outside the booth; she clearly looked more than aggravated with me by then. I, on the other hand, was getting extremely frustrated and irritated with my futile attempts. The operator, unaware of my predicament, still patiently but persistently kept telling me that she was waiting for me to begin inserting the correct number of coins into the proper slots.

She had no idea how I was hurrying frantically with no result, still struggling with my very first quarter, which simply refused to be pushed in. Then suddenly, quite accidentally, to my immense delight, like a miracle the quarter actually fell into the slot. Can you guess my amused reaction? "Oh wow! So that's how it works!"

Finally I made my connection with the wife of my dad's friend; I remembered them well from my childhood. Theodore was still at work; happy to get my call, she invited me to stay with them for the night to hear the latest news of my family. If I could take a commuters' train from a nearby local station to Crystal Lake, they would bring me back to Chicago the next morning for the continuation of my journey. Even though I was apprehensive to take up this new challenge, I still accepted their invitation.

It was one of those well-known, famously hot, Chicago days in late spring of '56. I asked, got the directions, and was assured that the terminal I needed to go to was within a short and easy walking distance.

With great difficulty I made my way on foot toward my destination, carrying a heavy winter coat, a large handbag, plus an overloaded and heavy overnight case. The street was an uphill climb; huffing and puffing, in that extreme heat, I was trying to walk as fast as I could with not much progress. Big drops of perspiration were running from my head down my face and back. I was extremely hot and feeling quite dehydrated. That wasn't such a short or easy walk after all.

I had been told by my cousins in the East that Chicago—I presume especially in those days—was a very dangerous place, and that I should not talk to or trust anyone, including the local police. As I was struggling to carry everything I had piled up on myself, I noticed two law enforcement officers walking together on the other side of the street. I was terrified to even look at them, much less ask them if I was walking in the right direction. If those policemen noticed me, at best they must have thought to themselves: "Here goes a weird individual bundled underneath a heavy winter coat in this scorching heat." At worst, they might have perceived me to be a highly suspicious character, desperatly trying to get away without looking in their direction, and was fearful to be noticed by them.

Finally, overheated and exhausted, I found the local commuters' station and boarded the right train on time; but still, I found myself a bit nervous since this was a side trip that was not on my agenda. I was afraid I would get lost or miss getting off the train at the correct station. So I found it quite reassuring when I heard the conductor calling out loudly the name of each upcoming station.

We got to Crystal Lake in forty-five minutes or so. My father's friend Theodore, with a big smile on his face, was already on the platform waiting for me. He took me to their home where I spent a wonderful evening with this lovely family; there his wife and mother had prepared a delicious, home-cooked meal fit for a queen—no comparison to a cheap, dry sandwich, which was the only thing I could afford on the train.

We talked over past cherished days long into the night, remembering humorous incidences and the love they shared with my family in years gone by. Later I was more than content to have had a quiet night's sleep in a clean and comfortable bed, and woke up the next morning wonderfully rested, to a delectable and nutritious breakfast. After many thanks and affectionate good-byes, my dad's friend drove me back to Chicago; there he personally helped me get on board the Santa Fe for Fresno. So I found myself back on a train again, still moving westward.

The next two days on the train I had plenty of time to daydream, listening to every metallic and rhythmic clanking of the wheels. Periodically the train's rocking motion would lull me to sleep, and then occasionally with its long, loud, high-pitched whistle, it would rudely wake me up. I could sense strongly that each *Choo-Choo* was taking me farther and farther from my home and family.

In the middle of the last night of the three-day trip, I was awakened from my light sleep as the train slowed down considerably, then came to a full stop at a small, rundown station which seemed to be in the middle of nowhere. I had no idea how far we had come or which state we were in; I assumed—and, I might add, thought brilliantly—that we were somewhere between Chicago and Fresno. But where were we?

At that hour of the night there was nothing moving on the platform. Even though it was pitch-black and slightly foggy I could still see, but faintly, the outline of a beat-up, barnlike terminal with a soft, blue light flickering at the top, far corner of its roof. With the searching eyes of a young detective and the vivid imagination of a teenager, I kept looking around to see if there was anything hiding in the surrounding shadows.

Aha! There it was. Underneath that dim nightlight I saw the silhouette of a man standing on one leg, reclined backward with his other foot well-planted on the wall of the old construction behind him; he was totally motionless as if in deep sleep. His huge, Western hat was pulled more than halfway down his face, and a lit cigarette was hanging from his lips. He was wearing knee-high boots, the perfect image of a cowboy, a leading man in a classic scene from an old Western movie. Could this be the stop at Death Valley? Intrigued by this scene, my theatrical mind was busy making up stories.

Still mesmerized, I was staring at this mysterious man, wondering what he was doing there all alone with no apparent purpose or destination in mind, when slowly but surely, without warning, the train started moving ahead again. Even the sound of the moving train did not budge this character; he stood there like a dummy in a wax museum. As we pulled away from the station, I felt sorry for the poor, lonely guy. So I wished the old cowboy sweet dreams and a good night, even though he had to sleep standing in a dreary, lonely corner.

I felt most fortunate for my own circumstances. Perhaps I was to spend another uncomfortably tiring night sleeping lightly, seated on a scarcely padded, slightly reclined chair; still, I felt secure and sheltered in the train; and best of all, I would not be standing on my feet all night like that pitiful fellow.

Early the following morning, the train stopped at Fresno's Station; I had come to my final destination . . . beautiful, sunny California! This was the place I had dreamt of and longed to be for so long. Now I could wake up from my dreams! At last, I was here in California; my home away from home!

Lord, I thank you, for you kept me safe during my long journey. Please stay and be with me always.

Chapter Five

Life in California

Almost a month later, literally thousands of miles away from home and family, and at the end of my very long journey loaded with new and exciting experiences, at last I reached my final destination. Here in Fresno, my life was at the threshold of a promising future.

I was happy to see the lovely wife of our former pastor already at the train station when we arrived. She was a saintly, soft-spoken, gentle soul; she took me directly to their home, where I was to stay as a guest for a short while. It was wonderful to be reunited with their two daughters; we were contemporaries and had been friends since childhood.

Here I was with people who knew my parents well for nearly twenty-five or thirty years; their past warm and sincere relationship made me feel close to my own family. They were welcoming and kind to me, so from the very first moment their genuine hospitality made me feel comfortable and at home. What a wonderful way to start my new life in a new land.

I was amazed and delighted to find out that, within their community, the pastor and his wife had met a few relatives of my maternal and fraternal grandparents. Before my arrival, I had no idea that in Fresno I was to find distant family members who had migrated from Turkish Armenia to Fresno at the turn of the century; I was happy to be taken to their homes for our first introduction.

I specifically remember one of my grandfather's first cousins, an elderly lady, who wept openly when we met. Grandpa had been like a brother to her before their families had dispersed all over the world during the Armenian genocide, which coincided with the First World War. Two generations had passed since, and here I was, one of the granddaughters to her cousin she adored most. I had awakened in her sweet and cherished childhood memories of her yesteryears.

I thoroughly enjoyed a week or two staying in Fresno with this wonderful family. However, there was still a couple of summer months left before I had to formally register at the Bible College. This was the perfect time for me to visit Redwood City and meet my father's older brother, whom I never knew. My uncle had left for the States in 1921. My dad at fourteen had hoped to join him; but sadly, to his great disappointment, his dream was never realized.

I only knew of my uncle since my father often spoke longingly of their childhood. I had only seen pictures of him, his wife, and their daughter Joyce, my first cousin. They were the only extension of my own flesh-and-blood family, and now I was to spend the rest of the summer with them. This promised to be a very exciting and deeply emotional experience for me as well as for them.

At that time, Uncle had not seen his parents or any of his siblings for over thirty-five years. From my childhood on, everyone who knew my grandmother would repeatedly call me "little Mariam," saying that I was very much like her in looks and personality. Daily, I must have reminded Uncle of her, stirring in him memories of his mother and his youth.

My uncle's often teary eyes, always full of tenderness and love, were identical to my father's whom I adored; the way he looked at me often brought tears to my own eyes, since I missed my dad in the worst way. Aunty was his love, and Joyce, his daughter, was the joy and pride of his life.

When the bus pulled into their local Greyhound station, my cousin was already there waiting for me. The immediate warmth I felt from her was amazing; this was more like a reunion rather than a first meeting. From that moment on we became inseparable, like two peas in a pod, as Auntie continually kept reminding us.

Joyce, their only child, had grown up lonely without siblings. I, on the other hand, had left four sisters behind and missed them; instantly we became sisters in mind and spirit. Happily married, Joyce was ten years my senior; from the moment we met she took me under her wings, becoming my guardian and confidant. We spent quality time together, talking unceasingly and sharing things past, present, and future.

She was hungry to know all about our family, starting with Grandma and Grandpa. She had two uncles, two aunts, and their children back home. There was an obvious longing and emptiness in her heart, which I tried to fill up with detailed information of our extended family.

One morning my fun-loving cousin drove the two of us up to San Francisco; in that single day, we went around to see all of the touristic landmarks unique to the beautiful city, built on Seven Hills. We saw the famous cable cars moving up and down the almost vertical streets, the legendary Gump's Department Store, the majestic Golden Gate Bridge, the Fisherman's Wharf, where we stopped for lunch, the Marina, and of course the one and only colorful and exciting Chinatown. She pointed out Alcatraz Island with its most famous prison, which since then has become a national historic landmark. I was exhilarated and exhausted, but that whole day was truly memorable and one of the most exciting experiences of my life to date.

But the most unexpected and unforgettable thing Joyce pulled on me occurred one morning quite early.

While I was still in deep sleep, she threw the blankets off of me—this was a perfect rise-and-shine moment—pulled me physically up and out of bed, and in a few short minutes, she was driving me to the appointment she had already made for a hair permanent. No cousin of hers was going to attend school in the States without a good hairdo!

Joyce was a sincere believer, a piano teacher, the choir leader and pianist of their church since her college days. I too loved music and had taken piano lessons from my childhood, plus voice lessons of late; I was also on my way to a small, church-affiliated college to major in sacred music. We had bonded immediately, shared everything, listened to and made music, laughed and cried together. That was one of the shortest, most carefree, and happiest summers I had in all of my student days.

Fall came too soon for me that year; before long I had to return to Fresno, present myself to the dean of the college, and register. At the end of the previous school calendar, the president of this small, private institute had received an introductory letter from my father concerning me. He in turn had read it to the whole school of approximately 150 students to prepare them for my arrival.

When classes resumed that fall, they all knew that among them was a young woman from Egypt living in the women's dormitory. I am almost sure I was the first foreign student to date attending that school, so their acute curiosity and wonderment were perfectly understandable.

Since I was basically very shy, I scarcely talked to anyone; for several days I lived quietly among them, ate with them in the dining hall, went to classes, and attended daily chapel. No one recognized me as the overseas student until I opened my mouth and spoke with a strong foreign accent intermingled with British pronunciation, leftover from my English high school days.

This was even more confusing and enigmatic to my fellow students since I did not look Egyptian. They had all expected to see someone wearing Middle Eastern Arab garb and Yemeni shoes, walking around with partially covered face. No wonder they did not recognize me as the foreign student; I did not fit their mental picture of an Egyptian.

Some of them thought that the first order of things for me was to have gone to J.C. Penney and bought the dress I was wearing. The fact that my dress code was no different from theirs was baffling enough; but it was further amazing to them to learn that I actually had made my outfit.

Initially, I was astonished at their totally different expectations. Why would an Arab attend a Christian Bible school? Many times I told them that I was an Armenian—Armenians, the first nation that accepted Christianity in history. Then they got truly confused trying to figure it out theologically, thinking of the difference between Arminianism and Calvinism. I was not an Egyptian but an Armenian born in Egypt; an Egyptian citizen but not an Arab. This was totally incomprehensible to them; how can one not be an Egyptian if one is born in Egypt? This was what they kept asking.

It didn't take me very long to realize this important fact: that even though most of the students were of German heritage, they disregarded that fact; they all equated birthplace, citizenship, nationality, ethnicity, and identity. For them, these were all one and the same thing. What they had was a totally Western concept, contrary to European or Middle Eastern, where first and foremost you are identified by your family's ethnicity, background, and heritage. Their logical argument they kept repeating was: "When born in America, you are an American, so . . ."

No amount of effort and endless discussions on the subject made any difference; this was a totally new and foreign concept. Even detailed explanations made no sense to them. Finally, after a few weeks, I figured out how to solve this enigma.

One day when this subject came up again, I had a small group of my fellow students around me. I asked them if their parents had been missionaries in the Far East and they had been born in either China or Japan, would their birthplace make them Oriental with dark, slanted eyes? Guess what, they finally got it!

Lord, I thank you for new friends and new opportunities.

Chapter Six

East Meets West

After a few weeks when we all got to know one another a little better and felt more relaxed with each other, many further questions came up concerning my ethnicity, family upbringing, and our lifestyle back home. I found some of their questions amusing and yet so sweet. They were wondering if my father had needed a translator to write out, type, and send the letter which was read to them by the president of the institute at the end of the previous school year.

Since I was coming from Egypt, had I seen the pyramids? How big and where in the desert was our tent located? How many camels did my father have? And did I ever ride one? Etc. Yes, I had seen the pyramids and the Sphinx too.

They couldn't believe that my father spoke several languages, had his own desk and typewriter, and was more than capable of writing his own letters in English. We did not live in the desert inside a big tent, but in one of the three luxurious apartments of our family-owned residential building in a large cosmopolitan city called Alexandria. This beautiful, historic city was built right on the coastline of the Mediterranean Sea; furthermore, my father drove an American-built Chevrolet instead of riding a one-hump camel.

These facts were all true, but for my newfound friends, it all sounded inconceivable. Together we used to chuckle over the contrasting pictures. But who could have blamed those young students; they had not traveled much, if at all, outside the United States. (Remember too, this was in the mid-fifties.)

Concerning Egypt, perhaps all they were exposed to was the most advertised, typical touristic places: scenes from documentaries, photography, or some collection of ancient artifacts in museums. I am sure they were well aware of the legendary River Nile; camels traveling in the desert; the Sphinx, the mysterious, stone-built marvel, half-woman, half-beast, which seems to be sitting there in the hot sands forever; and of course the famous pyramids tirelessly, continuously, and proudly reaching up to the heavens.

Many of them had probably seen the unforgettable pictures of tall palm trees, overloaded with huge, hanging clusters of fresh dates by the river and its fertile soil; farmlands, with cows and other animals grazing nearby; oxen, practically blindfolded, going round and round grinding wheat kernels. Nearby, there is a peasant woman washing clothes at the edge of the river with her children swimming nearby; and a farmer working his field with primitive tools, or drawing up buckets of water from a well for his family's daily use.

Those typical realities in the minds of my school friends were all logical, except they were not the whole picture, and were deficient in many important facts. They were not taught, nor had any concept, that Egypt had a very long and rich historic past. Ancient Egypt was one of the cradles of earliest civilizations. Its contributions to the world and society in medicine, astronomy, mathematics, and science are well documented.

Then and now Egypt has two large, old, and vital cities: Cairo and Alexandria. The Egyptian University, the National Museum, and the Opera House of Cairo, which was built for the premier of Verdi's *Aïda*, are all world renowned. Also in those days the Cairo Zoo was quite famous, well-known and admired all over for having the most attractive grounds and the largest collection of African animals anywhere. The Alexandria beaches were considered the most beautiful of any on the Mediterranean Sea coastline, including those of the European rivieras.

These two major cities were throughout history inhabited by innumerable nationalities from over the entire world. All these peoples from different origins, generation after generation, had lived there for thousands of years; they all had built schools, communities, and churches, including the Americans who besides churches and schools had built the American

University of Cairo. They were surprised that not only was I a graduate of an English school, but that earlier my mother also had graduated from the American mission school in Alexandria.

One evening I asked some of them if they would like to see my home movies, which I had brought over as a keepsake of my birthplace and family. Boy! What an eye-opener that was for all who came. After seeing what I had left behind, they then began to feel sorry for me for having chosen what they perceived was the lesser of the two lifestyles. I explained to them that though sometimes I felt terribly homesick, yet there were no regrets, and no thoughts of ever going back. This was simply God's leading in my life. This they understood.

It was wonderful when eventually they all felt free to tease me. First and foremost they picked on my accent. At every meal in the dining hall I could hear echoes of my words traveling down the table from student to student. "Plleezz puss de buttterr!" "Plleezz puss de wotterr!" "Plleezz puss de brredd!"

It didn't take long for me to copy and imitate the way they spoke. So one day, much to their amusement and surprise, I decided to exaggerate the California slur as I asked for certain eatables during a meal. The whole table went hysterical with laughter.

By now they had all realized that I was brought up in two large, culturally alive cosmopolitan cities;

therefore they decided that since I was a city girl, I probably had not seen farm animals—perhaps not even a cow. Conceivably I was not familiar with farm-fresh produce either, whereas many of them because of their rural background from all over California were quite knowledgeable with everything that pertained to a farm.

So one day, my best friend Zoe Ann, with whom I still correspond, left herself wide open to be teased by me in front of the whole dinner table. That turned out to be one of the most unforgettable meals we ever had during which I put on my best acting hat on and spoke loud enough to get the attention of everyone seated with us. Soon they were all quiet and were listening to our conversation.

As I was helping myself to a bowlful of salad, with a genuine, naive expression, pointing to a morsel of lettuce, I pretended to know nothing about it and asked my dear friend what that thing was. Further-more, I wanted to know if tomatoes grow on trees as potatoes do.

They all took me seriously, but unfortunately Zoe Ann, my lovely, sweet friend, was the one that fell into the trap; looking at me with empathy for my ignorance, and with great compassion in her voice, she went into a long, detailed dissertation. "Head lettuce," she explained, "is a round, fresh vegetable which grows on the ground. When ready it is picked up and sold to a grocery store; later, it is bought and chopped up for salads." Besides, she went on to say, neither tomatoes nor potatoes grow on trees.

For a long time I kept up the masquerade, but then a slight hint of a smile betrayed my mischievous—better call it naughty—behavior. We were all laughing heartily. Poor Zoe Ann, embarrassed, realized that the whole thing was a joke! After that the only thing she could say was, "Sometime, somewhere, somehow, I will get even with you."

Just a few years ago, with our husbands, Zoe Ann and I had a wonderful reunion in California; it was priceless to see each other again and evoke the past after forty years and some.

For the first year of my schooling I lived in the dormitory. What made the continuation of my musical education possible was the full, three-year scholarship, some financial support for living expenses, plus the administration's generous offer of a part-time job on campus.

My earlier prediction and the pronouncement I had made to my mother, concerning my willingness to work, came true from the start. However, I made sure she never heard of it; it would have killed her to know that her pampered, darling daughter, whom she raised to be a lady with art, music, and song, was now washing dishes in the kitchen of the school, cleaning the bathrooms and shower stalls for forty dormitory girls. My mother would have given anything if she could have changed the law and been able to send regular monetary support.

In the second year I left the dormitory life and moved in with an Armenian family, a young, working couple with two children. They had a very small house, so the back porch became my bedroom, with the dirty laundry basket lying next to an army cot where I slept. For a small weekly pay I was responsible for taking care of the whole household: cooking, cleaning, washing, ironing, and attending to the children's needs.

At home these were considered the most menial jobs that were held by the least educated individuals. More than a decade passed before my mother knew of this, my latest venture. During that year, I was carrying a full load at the school, and had achieved all A's in my studies. When did I have time to practice and study? How did I ever manage the pressures I was under? That is truly beyond my own comprehension!

My third and final school year, I was invited to live in with and be, more than anything else, a companion and caregiver to a kind and bright elderly Armenian lady, for the same weekly pay. In reality, it was the other way around; this wonderful woman who was acutely arthritic took care of me. She had a new extension added to her house with a beautifully furnished bedroom; a comfortable, plush bed; and a private bath; which was all to be mine while living with her.

She already had a cleaning lady who came in once a week. My duties were periodically, if needed, light dusting and vacuuming, helping her in and out of her bathtub, and accompanying her to the beauty shop in a cab for her weekly hairdo. And that was all.

Every day when I got home from school, quite contrary to my experience of the previous year, she was the one who had a delicious, hot meal ready for me. This beautiful lady, whom I ended up calling "Auntie," took great pleasure in watching me savor every morsel of her delicious cooking. Things were quite different now; instead of me taking care of her, it was actually Auntie who took care of and mothered me.

At the end of that school year I had to leave Fresno to continue my studies. Auntie and I had a warm and emotional parting. Just before I left, she predicted and clearly foresaw great achievements in my future.

In my first year at the Bible college, our choir director had arranged a spring concert tour up and down the West Coast; that is, from British Columbia down to the tip of Southern California. Driving along the Pacific Coast highway one beautiful mile after another is one of the most exquisite drives in all of nature. That travel and concertizing experience alone was a great education for us all.

Wherever we went, in local houses of worship, we performed oratorios such as Joseph Haydn's *Creation* and Felix Mendelssohn's *Elijah*; and at night we were welcomed as guests in the homes of church members. Some of the most wonderful anthems, oratorios, and other sacred works I have had the privilege of learning and performing were during those memorable few, short years.

Besides liberal arts courses throughout those years, I also took organ instructions, pursued with great enthusiasm my piano and voice lessons, and regularly participated in every recital. The highlight of my pianistic achievement came at the end of my third year, when I performed the first movement of Camille Saint-Saëns Piano Concerto no.2 in G minor. For the orchestral score, we substituted my piano teacher's organ accompaniment; that was exciting and fun.

Our choir director was also my voice teacher, as well as my guidance counselor. He and his wife, a loving couple, were very helpful to me personally and professionally; we became lifelong friends. After three years of being nurtured by them and all that the institute had to offer, upon their advice I went away with mixed feelings to continue my musical studies at The Conservatory of San Francisco.

This was a scary and important step forward. Once again I was to move into an unknown territory. I would uproot myself all over again, settle in a different city, attend a different learning institution, have different instructors, and make new and different friends all over again. It was time for a major change in every aspect of my life, and also was time again to pray for wisdom and guidance from above.

Dear Lord, you have brought me safely thus far. Please direct each forward step that I must take.

Chapter Seven

Moving to San Francisco

The compassionate and divine, invisible hand of God was directing my path once again. Transferring as a student with a double major was arranged for me with no difficulty, and without an audition my scholastic standing made my transition smooth and unproblematic. Again I was given a full scholarship plus part living expenses, without which it would have been impossible for me to continue my education; moreover, I would have lost my student's status and gotten into a serious problem with the immigration authorities.

While in temporary accommodations, by some curious circumstance in a week's time I was introduced to a young, working, Christian couple who had a lovely home in San Bruno, quite a distance from the city. It was not to be believed; they were looking for a young music student—and that happened to be me—to live in with them to do some light housekeeping, and in return they would provide her with room and board. There are no coincidences, and there are no accidents, right?

So they took me in. The husband happened to be a PhD candidate at the conservatory, so I had door-to-door daily transportation back and forth to my classes with him. This was simply the best and most wonderfully perfect arrangement; they were honest, kind, and quite fond of me; we simply got along beautifully. When God opens a door and leads, all obstacles vanish.

I was more than happy to be in a music conservatory atmosphere. It seemed to me I was in the right place at the right time. From the first day, private teachers were assigned to me. My piano teacher was an Italian master with a noteworthy reputation; he was very much impressed with my musicality and my aptitude for mature interpretations. His advice was that since piano was my second major, I would benefit greatly if in the first year we would exclusively concentrate on my technical skills. That suggestion was most agreeable to me. After several months I was pleased to see a notable improvement in my playing ability.

In the area of my vocal studies, for a few months things went on beautifully. It seemed to me everything was progressing satisfactorily; apparently not so for my instructor. Unfortunately, not everything that seems just right lasts; indeed, what happened next was most upsetting. One particular morning the day began quite normally, but by noon, my whole world had turned upside down.

During my voice lesson that day, I felt I died a little as I heard my own teacher cruelly cut me to the core, even though he thought he was being thoughtful and honest for my benefit. The one I trusted to help me improve vocally simply told me, without empathy or sensitivity, that my voice had no bottom or top register; I had only one-octave range in the middle of my voice, for which he said there was no repertoire written. In other words, I had no voice to speak of.

Speechless, I stood there for a few seconds; I could not believe what I had just heard. Then I left the room numb, disoriented, and in shock. Like a zombie without any feelings whatsoever, I walked in a daze directly into the registrar's office, which was next door down the hall.

I remember telling her plainly, void of any emotion, that I was quitting voice lessons. The response I got from the registrar, without giving me a chance to say another word, astounded me. Her immediate reaction was truly amazing. "So you want to stop singing, do you? Just because one person told you, 'You have no voice,' you came to that decision, did you? During and after others' voice lessons I regularly need aspirins. Your singing is the only one that does not give me a headache. And you are quitting on me? No, no way!" Bless her soul!

Immediately, she picked up the phone and arranged an audition for me with the conservatory's elderly, respected, and experienced Opera School director, who after hearing me sing only a couple of phrases from an aria by Mozart gave me his analytical and firm opinion.

His absolute conviction was that my voice was a young dramatic soprano, which is known as a "Spinto." He went on to explain that at my age, that category of voice happens to be in its infancy, and because of it, is still in the process of developing. He also mentioned that dramatic voices are rare, and therefore most teachers do not know what to do with them, how to nurture or train them. He added that if I had known better and were given a choice, I would have asked God exactly for this type and quality of voice.

He said his piece, and on his way out the door he added: "Find a better teacher for yourself." And then he was gone! His final and only suggestion was short, sweet, and to the point; no arguments, no discussions. Talking about becoming confused! I was given two acutely contradictory opinions concerning my voice in a matter of two days.

Soon after that the registrar assigned me to a different vocal instructor who very carefully and painstakingly worked with me exclusively on vocal technique for the rest of the school year. What we achieved together in the following months resulted in a remarkable improvement in my voice. I finally began feeling confident and happy again with the transformation I was hearing in my own voice. I was flying high!

To crown my latest thrilling triumph at the close of that school year, I received a letter from my father congratulating me for the past several years of successful schooling. He also strongly suggested that I should use part of the money they had managed to send over, to fly to Montréal and spend the summer months visiting my older sister. She was by then married, moved and had settled in Canada with her husband and their three-year-old daughter.

I had not seen any of my family for over four years; truly this was exciting and a great gift I could not refuse, so I left for Canada right after the last day of school. This promised to be a wonderful reunion since my older sister and I were very close emotionally, in age and size as well; most of the time we were thought to be twins. I knew her husband as well from our church's young peoples' group, and now I was to meet the newest member to our family, my beautiful baby niece.

Just a few days after my arrival, one early morning I found my sister alone in tears over her first cup of coffee. She was depressed that I had to return to California after my short visit. Adding to her distress was the fact that in the attempt of immigrating to Canada, the rest of our close-knit family had become fragmented.

I was on the West Coast of the United States, she was in Eastern Canada, my father with our two younger siblings was in Lebanon, and my mother with the youngest one was still in Egypt. That morning between sips of coffee and tears, my sister tried to persuade me to continue my studies in Canada. At least the two of us would be closer geographically, she reasoned. I was torn between her pleadings and my own conviction that my personal musical growth and future artistic development was in San Francisco.

It was not easy to forget the exciting vocal improvement I had made within the last few months, the result of hard work, sweat, and tears. Besides, I was happy in San Francisco; with the conservatory, my piano teacher, and most of all, my new singing teacher who had practically performed miracles with my voice! The whole idea of being uprooted again was not one that I cherished, so I sat down with my sister and talked things over at length.

"I left my heart in San Francisco" was the ideal song to have sung that morning . . . I was torn between my own hopes and dreams and my sister's logic. So instead of singing, I needed to have my intimate meeting with the One who loved and cared for me; he knew what was best for me.

I asked the Lord for his clear guidance in my thinking and decisions; either choice would permanently shape and alter the course of my whole future. If I was to return to the States, I needed his divine intervention in creating obvious obstacles for my stay; or else make the transition so smooth that there would be no doubt left which way I was meant to go. It was time again for the prayer I had used often for God's guidance.

Dear Lord, you have been with me so far. Please direct me; which way do you want me to go next?

During the previous four years in California I had practically forgotten the little French I knew; besides, the French spoken in Montreal was totally foreign to me. So we seriously considered Toronto as a practical solution. That would not be too bad; I had uncles, aunts, and cousins galore that had already established themselves there, and that was not too far from Montreal.

There was no trouble transferring my grades and modifying my foreign student's status to Canadian. I took that as a clear, green sign, and so at the end of that summer, I moved to Toronto and stayed a few weeks with relatives. Whatever personal things I had left behind in California were shipped to me. There was no looking back now, and so my move had became permanent.

Unbeknownst to all of us, there were two established music institutions in Toronto: The Royal Conservatory, and the Faculty of Music of the University.

Even though it was clear from my documents that I was a straight A student with full scholarships for four consecutive years, this still left no impression on nor made a difference to the powers that were in Canada.

An audition was a must and an absolute requirement; I had to be tested and evaluated in order to be accepted and eligible for registration at either school of learning.

I had always performed better than auditioned, but this time that did not matter. In the previous year in San Francisco, I was kept solely on technique in both venues; my repertoire for these tryouts was practically nonexistent. Besides, for months, that is from late spring to early fall, I had had no instruction, also had no access to a keyboard, therefore I had not practiced piano or done any singing. Totally rusty and ill-equipped, trapped in my own circumstances, I had no choice but go through a mockery of the evaluations. This was when the second shoe fell, and fall it did, royally: right on my head.

Dear God, now what?

Chapter Eight

Canadian Trials and Tribulations

At the appointed day, when I walked onstage I was feeling quite insecure and unprepared for the required auditions. Halfway up the auditorium I saw several individuals seated with pad and pencil looking quite formal. Later I found out that among the adjudicators were the Director of the Royal Conservatory and the Head of the Faculty of Music of the University of Toronto.

After what was my worst and most excruciating experience in auditioning both in piano and voice, I heard those same devastating, disparaging words over again. This time they were more explicitly expressed than before. I was well aware that I had not auditioned well, which was painful enough, but to listen to their clearly articulated verbal evaluation at the end of my audition was unspeakably unbearable. It was as if there was not a shred of salvageable or a hint of musical aptitude in me. Their words left me utterly crushed. I was told most definitely and in plain language: "It is better for you to be told now rather than in ten years that you are and have been pursuing the wrong profession. You have absolutely no pianistic or vocal talent, and therefore you should look for a different vocation in life."

That indeed felt like the straw that broke the camel's back. Up to that time I had been continuously a student in excellent standing with the highest of marks; I also received awards above and beyond the full scholarships for four consecutive years from two different institutions, specifically for my musical abilities. Now I was being told I was not gifted in either venue.

Their choice of words which were clearly a total dismissal of me and my talents seemed unreal, heartless, and cruel, especially right after the agonizing discouragement I had gone through in San Francisco just the year before. Their evaluation felt like an assault on my psyche and spirit.

Dear Lord, what just happened?

I remember walking out of that building totally devastated, stumbling as in heavy fog, unaware of my surroundings, dragging one foot after the other as if in a trance, a lost soul moving forward without a specific direction.

I have no idea how long I was in that stupor and how far I had wandered, when suddenly it was as if a bolt of lightning jolted me to awareness. I heard the shrieking, deafening noise of the brakes of a cable car which had stopped in the nick of time and the hysterical shouts of swear words from the panic-stricken conductor; I was effectively shocked into self-awareness.

When I regained my senses, I found myself between the tracks of the oncoming streetcar, standing there with wide-open, glassy eyes just two feet from the stopped trolley, and closest ever to my imminent demise. I have no recollection as to how I got myself back onto the sidewalk; I was petrified, stunned, and shaken, self-conscious under the disparaging stares of the crowd. Never was I so traumatized in my life; I had completely lost awareness of who or where I was.

I stood there on the sidewalk trying to hold myself together, trembling for a long while until I managed to find my equilibrium. Somehow, eventually complete realization took over; I knew beyond a shadow of doubt that I could easily have died that very day. Grateful to be alive, I reminded myself that life was far more valuable than music, which had filled and taken over my existence.

Lord, thank you for sparing my life.

But what was I to do now? I was deeply depressed. Rejected by both musical institutions, my hopes were crushed; the door to my future had been slammed shut and bolted. Unfortunately, by then my bridges back to the States were also burnt. I felt totally devastated and ruined. To further complicate my situation, I was on a student's visa and could no longer remain in Canada unless I became a full-time student. But study what?

The only love of my life was music, and that was taken away from me. Change my major? Change it to what? Even hair dressers' school in Toronto would not have accepted me because I did not have the equivalent of Ontario's grade thirteen. I felt miserable and thoroughly lost!

I couldn't quite understand why things were going so badly for me. This was the Lord's leading, wasn't it? I had come to accept it as such, so why these difficulties and this impossible situation now?

This was not my idea of going forward. You can believe that in my deep frustration I had a long list of questions for God. He seemed to have smoothly arranged my transfer, but then soon after, I found myself to be on a dead-end road.

> *Lord, where are you now, when I need you? Are you aware of my present situation? Do you see what is happening to me? Are you genuinely concerned when I am hurting so? Lord, where are you leading me now? Or are you still leading me? Have you changed your*

*mind concerning me and your will for
me? Do you really, truly care? Lord, are
you sure you know what you are doing?*

He seemed, oh, so distant, deaf, and silent. Even
though I questioned him like an ignorant child in
desperate frustration, shame, and humiliation, down
deep I knew my Father in heaven always knew what he
was doing, but I surely did not understand any of this.

From my own perspective, it seemed that I unexpectedly, abruptly, was pushed and forced off the track
I was on. This was worse than being simply derailed;
I was made to maneuver a sudden and sharp U-turn
most unwillingly. I had nothing to say about it, and
had no control over any of it.

The thought of going all the way back to a new starting point for a completely different life's journey was
like having a nightmare. All of my hopes and dreams
were utterly shattered. In desperation I cried:

*O God, where are you? Do you hear my
cry? Why is this happening to me? You
feel so distant to me.*

Chapter Nine

Finding a New Home

It is easy to remain strong in faith when things are smoothly going our way. But when we are crossing troubled waters, it is indeed difficult to keep on believing that God in his wisdom and infinite love always is mindful of us. When we can't see the road ahead, he does. No matter how we perceive things, God knows the truth of the situation. We might not know what tomorrow holds, but should remember who holds tomorrow. If we believe and trust him, we must keep in mind that he is constantly working behind the scenes for our benefit. This definitely is not an easy lesson to learn.

Looking back, in hindsight I can see now that God in his wisdom intentionally, temporarily was changing my circumstances and dramatically altering the direction I was moving in, in order to shape my future according to his specific plan for my life.

Who among us has faith strong enough to bear in mind at each and every crucial time in our lives to rest in the Lord and relax with confidence, knowing that our loving God is in control and in time will turn our painful failures into incomparable successes, beyond what we could ask or even imagine? It is still true . . . *"All things work together for good to those who love God"* (ROMANS 8:28 NEW KING JAMES VERSION).

In this terrible predicament, I was still quite fortunate that one of my cousins helped me with the emigration authorities. Since the university had turned me away, to save my student's status with the Canadian authorities, I had to be registered in an accredited school as a full-time student. Within a couple of weeks he had me registered in yet another Bible college; since I couldn't return to the States, I had nowhere else to go, except perhaps back to Egypt. I was trapped.

But this felt all wrong, discouraging, demoralizing, and painfully regressive. I had no remorse or guilt for missing most of my classes. I was in the wrong place at the wrong time; I had been there and done that in the past; I needed to go forward. I felt completely lost. The experts had told me to give up music, and who was I to argue with their judgment? Their rejection of me was one of the most agonizing experiences of my life.

Several weeks later I had moved into the downtown area and was living in a room at the home of a middle-aged spinster, an artist in watercolors. She was very nice, but her aging cat regularly, overnight, would leave several messes on the kitchen floor. So each morning I had to walk zigzagging on tiptoe to cross the width of the kitchen to get to the coffeepot. Eventually I opted to forgo my morning coffee and breakfast.

Totally miserable with my lot in my life, professionally and personally, I was continuously questioning the Lord as to his doings and then the undoing of his plans for my life; I didn't understand any of this. How long did I have to wait? I needed and wanted answers from him, and soon. I must admit shamefully that there were times I thought he had totally forgotten me. Even so, I could not afford to let him go. He was my only recourse and my only deliverance from all that was wrong in my life.

The fall season soon had changed into the Canadian winter. Family and friends, who themselves had emigrated from Egypt and had already lived through several winters in Toronto, all had tried unsuccessfully to prepare me for the extreme cold I was to experience. I am afraid the severity of it had not sunk deep enough into my grasp.

Having been brought up in the Egyptian desert heat, then basking for years in California's sunny, warm climate, all my life I had known nothing but hot weather. It was not too difficult to imagine the cold, but freezing? Now, the first order of the day was to buy some warm clothes, most specifically a warm coat and hat, a pair of gloves, and also my very first pair of waterproof boots lined with heavy wool.

A couple months, maybe three, went by. In the midst of living in this limbo, facing an uncertain, seemingly dark and foreboding future; unhappy with my living quarters; feeling utterly broken up at the merciless turn of events in my personal life; God's unseen hand reached down once more to help and guide.

A cousin of my mother's, Albert, concerned about my predicament, under the pretence of their need for me called and invited me to visit him and his family, over that weekend. He came downtown and picked me up that very afternoon.

Within a few days Albert, his wife, Angel, and their teenage daughter took me in as a member of their family. I was treated as a second daughter in every way imaginable; they became my surrogate parents, and I found a second home away from home. That seemingly short, temporary visit lasted five whole years.

I had not realized until then that in the previous four years of my schooling in the States, while pursuing my studies and embracing excitedly all the new experiences life was generously bestowing on me, I had become too busy and preoccupied to be aware that I was in an emotional starvation mode for family life and support.

In a few short weeks after I had moved to Canada, the solid ground and the road I was traveling on had experienced a major earthquake; I felt the firm foundation I was building my future on collapsing and breaking into unredeemable pieces. As concerned and deeply troubled as I was about my personal situation, there in my cousin's home I found comfort, stability, encouragement, nurturing, and a sense of belonging that I absolutely hungered for and desperately needed. God in His wisdom provided again what I needed most, just in the nick of time.

> *Thank you, Father, for you do take care of me.*

After I moved in with my cousin's family, I permanently stopped going to the Bible school where I was registered, and out of necessity I also gave up all musical involvements. Even though I felt their warm welcome, was secure and content at my cousins, I still could feel a void in my life like a huge hole. I was convinced and mourned the fact that the past four years, with all the struggles that I had endured and unlimited efforts I had spent to accomplish my dreams, were a total loss, entirely a waste of time.

Yet, in hindsight, perhaps this was exactly what I needed at that particular time in my life: to come to a full stop in my marathon race for achievement, and accept some time off from everything that had taken over my life and consumed my energies. It was time to nurture my soul and spirit. I also earnestly tried to make peace with the hand that was dealt to me, reluctantly accepting failure; I patiently, humbly, and finally willingly began waiting on the Lord to see what his next plan was for me.

I was truly blessed that I was with cousins who were sincere believers, genuinely practicing their faith with spiritual maturity. My own spiritual growth in the five years I lived with them far exceeded that of my Bible school days of learning. Now in my midtwenties, I had become a very different young woman from the teenager who left the old country. Here in my new home and family I also felt truly loved, accepted, and appreciated for who I was, not merely for the talent that I might have had.

They understood the loss I felt and never ridiculed or made light of it—no time for a pity party for me! They were steadily encouraging and positive in their input. There was a lot of laughter, outings, and shared, meaningful family time; a healing process had begun in my soul. Though I missed music, especially singing, yet the acute edge of the pain I had felt was not as razor-sharp any longer; I was firmly convinced in my heart that in time, love and acceptance cure all ailments.

A year went by during which I became somewhat involved in the church, played for the Sunday services, and taught piano to some of the kids in the community. Life at my cousin's was comfortable and good. I had time now for more socialization like a normal person, and yet something huge was missing from my life. Was I to live the rest of my life with this empty feeling, without any passion for something that identified me? The mere thought of singing even in private made me uneasy and tense; it was as if I did not want to hear my own voice. But for how long? Where was this, my present condition, leading me?

> *Dear Lord, how long will I have to wait*
> *for your personal interest, involvement,*
> *and intervention in my life?*

Chapter Ten

Turn of Events; Try Again

We humans at best can perhaps see one step ahead of us at a time. Amazingly, with that limited ability, we often try to manipulate circumstances to pave our whole future. Even we who believe in God, his love and caring participation in our lives, at times become overly anxious because we are quick to forget past miracles and are slow to learn. Sometimes what we perceive to be his definitive plan or will for our lives is simply a passageway, only a walkway to get us to that specific, preordained place of his choosing where he had intended to take us all along. There we finally discover the ultimate purpose and destination of our lives.

When midway events and circumstances change the direction of our course, we tend to lose our faith in the One who knows the way, the place, and its timing better than us. That is precisely when we need to *"Rest in the Lord and wait patiently for Him"* (Psalm 37:7 NKJV), trusting in his love and grace, for God keeps his promises and will never fail us.

He gathers and shapes all things together; with a piece of humble clay, like a master sculptor, he creates a work of art uniquely beautiful. From the printed page of a symphonic work, like a great conductor, he brings out magnificent melodies with rich harmonies and makes heavenly music. Later, in great wonderment, we see that God was in control all along and in his great wisdom was preparing a superior plan for our lives. Life is truly a walk of faith. *"Be still, and know that I am God"* (Psalm 46:10 NKJV).

It took awhile longer, but in due time the turmoil of my soul subsided; I couldn't stay away from music much longer, particularly from singing. But where and how would I find a private teacher outside the conservatory? How much would my weekly lessons cost? And how would I pay for them?

Those were questions I had no answers for. I looked for and found different part-time jobs and worked whenever given the opportunity. Sadly, I was well aware that the income from them was hardly enough for the needed weekly lessons in the upcoming year. I knew no one who was knowledgeable in the music field, who could be helpful in giving me practical suggestions and a sensible direction.

The following summer, when visiting my sister back in Montréal, incredibly, I found a position to be a caregiver to a four-year-old boy who had just lost his mother. I was one of several helpers in the mansion of this recently widowed, wealthy gentleman. The abundant sum of the weekly pay he offered me was utterly unbelievable and absolutely unheard of. Miracles never cease!

Later I learned that this kind and generous man had become aware of my foreign student's status and the need of finances to keep up with my studies. Out of his benevolence he had wished personally to help me. Here was yet another total stranger that God used as an angel of mercy. What I could and did save that summer was more than enough to cover the expense of all my voice lessons for the whole upcoming year. At that point I needed to sing, sing just for my own pleasure and nothing else.

Come fall, back in Toronto, I found and worked with a voice teacher who after several months of lessons strongly advised and encouraged me to participate in the graduating, end-of-year vocal exam at the Royal Conservatory, which was open to all students for personal evaluation and eventual certification. This had nothing to do with being a full-time, registered undergraduate at the conservatory. Naturally I was extremely hesitant, but she was quite confident I could do this and do it well.

Because of the last-minute and fast-approaching

deadline for applications, plus my limited familiarity of the required songs and arias from the specific listing for my voice category, having no other recourse, I had to select songs and arias from contralto, mezzo, and dramatic soprano repertoires. This was highly unorthodox; it is not to be encouraged by teachers or practiced by students who take their studies seriously.

Truthfully, at that time I had no choice; a desperate situation called for desperate measures. If nothing else, I was well prepared and felt quite secure musically and vocally, even though I was going to present a confused program at the exam. After a successful, final vocal exam, I would on my own review (since I had covered the material in the previous years) for the two required written tests; this would make me eligible for my certification in vocal performance from the conservatory.

In the following year I would also complete the two required piano exams and become a graduate of the Royal Conservatory with my double major. That would make me a well-qualified teacher even at the conservatory; my source of income would be guaranteed, and finally I would become monetarily independent. There it was: a small light at the end of the long, dark tunnel.

On the appointed day of my exam I was as nervous as a sick cat, especially when I walked onstage and saw unexpectedly the very same adjudicators from my earlier audition two years before. I almost fainted; there they were to evaluate me all over again.

During the whole time I was singing through my prepared program, instead of concentrating on the words and the musical interpretation of the songs (which is absolutely critical and just as essential, if not more, than vocal technique at that age), my mind was frantically racing, working overtime in panic, wondering what these men were thinking of my audacity to have the nerve to appear again in front of them; had they not told me in no uncertain terms to forget music altogether?

I have no clear recollection as to how satisfactory or unacceptable I sounded. All I remember was that I was more than nervous and tense, the two fatal enemies that no one should have to deal with while performing. I desperately wanted to get through my songs, walk off that stage as fast as I could, and go into a permanent hiding place. Mercilessly they made me sing my entire program before they let me go. Perhaps the hodgepodge collection of my chosen vocal pieces made them more than suspiciously curious.

Afterwards my accompanist, who had worked with me diligently, told me confidentially how disappointed she was in my performance. She had heard me often enough to know that I could have and should have sung much better. Feeling deeply disappointed and unbearably defeated once more, I could not get home fast enough to mourn in private my repeated miserable failure.

Dear God, not again!

Chapter Eleven

Miracles Never Cease

For every dark cloud, at least a few of them must out of necessity have a silver lining; otherwise life at times would become agonizing and intolerable.

Right after my singing exam, I felt it to be once again a colossal defeat in my repeated attempts at what seemed an unattainable challenge; the sky overhead was totally blanketed with the most menacing darkness, without the slightest hint or ray of sunlight which might have been hiding behind it. I desperately tried but could not feel or see even a small flicker of hope in my future. What I needed most urgently was an honest-to-goodness, genuine miracle.

My life had become a continuous, nonstop routine of highs and lows, ups and downs, like a game of yo-yo. To have worked so hard, literally for years, with dedication and passion to finally achieve a set of goals, but after all the struggles to have miserably failed at it, was emotionally extremely tiring and discouraging.

I felt I was on a stationary bicycle paddling as fast as I could, or running nonstop in circles to the point of complete exhaustion, and yet getting nowhere. How disappointing and useless it was to have exerted all of my energies unproductively for so long, when all I wanted from the beginning was simply to go forward and attain some semblance of success.

Despondent and depressed, stooped under the burden of recurring defeat that was weighing heavily on my shoulders, I began seriously contemplating again, for the third and now most definitely the last time, giving up music for good. The thought of permanently, willingly, and personally closing this chapter of my life hurt to the depths of my soul; it was like deliberately letting a little bit of me die.

I esteemed my last performance for the examiners to be a total failure. Practically in tears, I rushed for home and got into a noisy, fast-moving subway. Even the earsplitting clamor of the train could not interrupt my troubling and disquieting thoughts. I was on my way back to my cousin's, for there was nothing else left for me to do and nowhere else to go.

By the time I got home, I had managed to work up a frightfully negative mood; I felt totally depressed and utterly hopeless. What was to become of me? Would

I forever be a failure? Where should I go from here, which way should I turn?

As soon as I entered the house, I felt the need to unburden my soul by telling my surrogate family all about my horrible experience of that miserable day. But I was not given a chance, for from the first moment I got in the door they informed me that there was an urgent message from Dr. Walter's office, and that I should return his call as soon as possible. Dr. Walter? What earthly reason would he have had to call me?

Dear Lord, what now?

Needless to say I became anxious, apprehensive, and curious at the same time. All of the adjudicators must have thought that I was stubbornly incorrigible with a healthy amount of ego to have come back for another try when they had told me in no uncertain terms to give up music altogether. Some nerve! I needed to sit down; my brain was racing with all kinds of nonsensical reasons for his call. Perhaps a well-deserved ridicule or possibly a severe reprimand for wasting their precious time was in order?

My hands were literally shaking when I picked up the phone; I desperately needed to calm down. After a moment or two of hesitancy, nervously I dialed the university number.

To my delight and immense surprise, the voice of the secretary at the other end was enthusiastic and cheerful. She said that at the end of a long list of applicants that morning, I was the last one to sing for Dr. Walter. Right after I had sung for them, Dr. Walter had come back to his office in a hurry, seeming quite excited. Instead of attending to the big pile of work on his desk that was waiting for him, the first thing he did was to tell her without delay: "Call that girl, the one from Egypt, and set up an appointment with her; I want to see her as soon as possible." Although unplanned and unintended, my insane, absolutely crazy list of exam pieces, compiled from the widespread selections of all three standard female voice categories, must have made the auditors sit up and take notice, to see if I satisfactorily possessed the wide vocal range needed to handle the extensive repertoire. Undoubtedly this alone impressed them all, most favorably. Was this a blessing in disguise, or what?

The very next day I found myself in the office of Dr. Walter, seated opposite his desk. He was an elderly Austrian gentleman, who at that moment held my future in his hands. I was sure beyond any doubt that he remembered me clearly from my earlier, miserable, unforgettable, and painful original audition. After the usual and normal greetings, I was having difficulty concentrating on what he was saying: "My dear, we don't generally make these kinds of mistakes in our judgments, but in your case, unfortunately, we made a dreadful one. I speak to you as a father; if you would give us three years of your time, we are prepared to offer you a full scholarship and part living expenses till you graduate with your Artist Diploma in vocal performance from the university. There are many horses that run in a race; I am betting my money on you. You have already lost two years; don't waste any more of your precious time. Please be wise and accept our offer."

Here was yet another angel in disguise. It was as if he was asking *me* to do *them* a favor. I sat there speechless, staring dumfounded at Dr. Walter's kind expression. For the first time I noticed his eyes; they had a twinkle in them, and his wavy, red hair had begun graying at the temples.

I was looking directly at and listening intently to him speaking to me with his beautifully clear Austrian accent, yet I was having a very hard time taking it all in. I could not quite comprehend or believe what I was hearing; I was not prepared for this amazing, miraculous turn of events. My mind was racing. "Did I hear him right? Did he actually say what I thought he said? Can this be true? This simply is not happening!"

My vocal exam was an evaluation for the secondary institution, the Royal Conservatory. But now the very same adjudicators who turned me away earlier were offering me a complete scholarship for three consecutive years, plus some living expenses.

They wanted to help me monetarily, educationally, musically, and therefore emotionally till I graduated from the Faculty of Music of the University, which was more prestigious than the conservatory.

Besides providing free weekly voice lessons, three years in the vocal program of the university automatically included opera schooling as well, which was run by the director of the Canadian Opera Company. As if that wasn't generous enough, as I was still sitting there in awe, Dr. Walter offered me an additional scholarship to continue with regular private piano lessons concurrently for the following three years.

I can't find words to express all the thoughts that were racing though my mind, the mixed feelings I was experiencing as I sat there stunned and looking unbelievingly at Dr. Walter's gentle face, which at the same time had a regretful expression.

This was an apology second to none, not in words alone but in deeds as well. After I recovered from the shock I was in, it took me only a few seconds to accept his offer with immense gratitude. I thanked Dr. Walter profusely, we shook hands, and I left his office walking on air.

Lord, thanks for miracles that renew our faith in your goodness.

Chapter Twelve

Canadian University Years

It was late spring, the end of that school year. After my successful vocal exam and unbelievable meeting with Dr. Walter, life as I knew it had made an incredible about-face. For the first time in a very long while, I felt hopeful and happy concerning my personal existence. In addition to my high spirits, I was looking forward to my return to Montréal to join my sister and our two younger siblings, who by then had immigrated and were staying with her and her family.

To top all of this excitement, I was experiencing an indescribable, deep anticipation, for in a few weeks the rest of our family, my parents and our youngest sister, after many months of innumerable difficulties, were finally coming to settle in Canada. After all the grueling preparations they had endured, they still had a very long flight ahead of them. We knew they would land in Montréal exhausted; all we wanted was their safe arrival.

So, on that day, we were all at the airport ahead of schedule. For me, the waiting for the arrival of their plane and the eagerness of our reunion, compared to my sisters, was by far more intense. More than seven years had passed since I had seen them last, and yet in a curious way, it seemed as if it was only yesterday. I yearned to see and hug them once again . . . Surely this reunion promised to be deeply emotional.

You can only imagine our excitement when it was announced that the plane which was bringing the last few members of our family had just landed. Sure enough, a little while later . . . which for us seemed endless . . . we saw them walk out of the double doors that separated us. This was their homecoming. We ran into each other's arms laughing and crying at the same time; oh! Such joy!

Yet within that celebration I felt my heart break, for I noticed my parents had visibly aged beyond their time in just a few short years. I am sure that, more than the lengthy travel, it was the pressures, concerns, and the fears they had gone through till they were granted their visas. They also had to leave behind practically everything they owned; that too must have taken its toll on them.

It was wonderful to have our whole family finally together again, and I had almost all of that summer to spend with them before returning to Toronto; I cherished the thought of having several weeks of quality time with them all. Those were thrilling and busy months, trying to make up for lost time, helping them acquire their basic needs, and settling them in an apartment of their own.

Soon fall was around the corner; once again it was I, who like the black sheep of the family, had to leave them all behind and move on to fulfill my dream; thankfully, this time it was a shorter distance away. By the end of August I had already returned to Toronto to start my three-year university course, grateful to take advantage of the incredibly generous gift of the scholarships. Finally, after so many turbulent years, I was going to complete my formal education.

During the next most unforgettable and fruitful three years at the University of Toronto, I was busy attending classes in music history, theory, form and analyses, besides Italian and French, German language and Lieder, stage deportment, private piano and voice lessons, plus opera school. I participated yearly in solo recitals and different opera productions.

Even as a child, I was told I acted well and looked quite natural on stage. Acting had become a passion, so my newest and most exciting venture was to join the Canadian Opera Company's chorus. It was fun to be in makeup and costume with all my newfound singer friends; we performed together in all of the operas for the next three seasons.

My various classes, practice hours at the piano, vocalizing, and time spent memorizing new repertoire kept me busy almost twenty-four hours a day. Like a dry sponge, I was drinking it all in. The music department was perhaps the smallest faculty on campus, and the voice majors seemed to be the smaller group within the smallest minority. We all worked very closely with each other and built genuine and lasting friendships.

How fortunate I was to be living with my cousins in those busy years. Each morning Albert would drive me downtown and drop me near the Faculty of Music building on his way to work. At home I had my private living quarters; when I came home after each long and tiring day, dinner would be ready and so were they.

They gave me their time, helped me to unwind, and allowed me to share with them my new experiences. What a privilege it was to have a place to come home to where I was loved, could relax from the pressures of the day, and be restored to some semblance of a normal life.

In my third and last year, among other operatic excerpts I also had performed a scene from the opera *Aïda* which was considered to be the highlight of the evening according to our opera school director. That same year, in midwinter, unbeknownst to me I had contacted and was infected with mononucleosis, plus had developed hepatitis. Several months went by before I became aware that I was feeling constantly and exceptionally tired, to the point of complete exhaustion.

I had been overworking, having just finished my final written exams and performed my last required recital for graduation. "Naturally this is to be expected," I thought to myself. These alone were good enough reasons for my extreme fatigue. When my eyelids became slightly swollen and my eyes turned red, the logical assumption on my part was that I had contracted the eye infection which was going around on campus.

But most frustrating was the fact that whenever I sang, I definitely felt there was something not quite right with my voice. Naturally, being so very tired was not helpful to a singer; I knew that for a fact. However, never having been in poor health before, I had no idea how dreadfully sick I was. The thought that I could be seriously ill did not even cross my mind. The glandular fever was causing havoc in my throat.

Around this time I was invited to sing in Montréal at an anniversary banquet at the church where my family attended. I took the Greyhound bus, and all the way for six to seven hours, I was sitting there itching and scratching all over; my eyes were puffy and bloodshot. When I arrived home, my mother thought I had been crying all the way from Toronto. I looked and felt horrible.

At the banquet hall the following evening, the aromas of food from the kitchen made me nauseous. By then I was feeling dizzy; the shiplike rocking of the banquet hall was making me seasick. Feeling unmistakably ill, I could barely sing half of my program. Right after my performance, I was taken home and went directly to bed. The next morning, my eyes betrayed the fact that I was also jaundiced.

The very same day, on Sunday afternoon, I was taken to our family doctor who was kind enough to take care of me at a moment's notice. His diagnosis was that I had a severe case of mononucleosis and a full-blown, dangerous level of infectious hepatitis, which naturally resulted in the jaundice. He immediately administered strong antibiotics, drew blood for complete detailed analysis, and, in addition, ordered total and strict bed rest for the rest of summer.

Again, after so many years, I was in the loving care of my parents. They were there night and day to make sure that their daughter was getting better. I never made it to my own graduation. Confined to bed, the only bright spot during those months was a beautiful get well card from Dr. Walter, with his handwritten message: "Congratulations for your Aïda performance. At convocation as I was watching your graduating class walk in to get their diplomas, I looked for your angelic face, but alas, you were not among them. Get well soon."

Later I found out that in all of his years at the university, Dr Walter had never, ever done anything resembling this gesture for any other student. This compassionate, generous man must have also realized that because of my physical condition, I could not have gotten the full benefit from my final year; so, as if still indebted to me, he provided again an additional complete scholarship for the following year, that is beyond graduation, for free, private piano and voice lessons, plus opera school for more stage experience. This was truly going beyond the second and even the third mile to make amends. I shall be eternally grateful to him. *God bless you, Dr. Walter!*

At the end of that summer, feeling somewhat better, I left for Toronto, back again to the university for that one extra year of post-graduate work, a gift from my benefactor, Dr. Walter. I knew full well, that particular year was to be formally and permanently the end of my student days. Out of necessity I had to face and undergo another huge, life-altering transition. So then what would I do? Where would I go? How would I make a living?

I was told to be patient and take things easy, and that it would take a little over a year to regain my normal strength after the terrible depletion of my energies. To add to my fragile health condition, perhaps because of the weakness of my immune system, soon I came down with a severe case of laryngitis, the worst thing that can happen to a singer when facing an impending performance.

I had an understudy who seemed not to have taken her responsibility seriously and was not prepared to step in for me. I begged the conductor of our university orchestra to have her take over my performances, but my pleadings fell on deaf ears and were totally useless.

I was told she was not ready to perform and that I had to go on. I also asked my own voice teacher for help. Much to my dismay, she could not or would not intervene. I was made to sing three performances of the character Smeraldine in Sergei Prokofiev's opera *The Love for Three Oranges* over a forty-piece orchestra, with a bad case of inflammation of my larynx and obvious hoarseness.

From that day on, after singing for a short while my voice would become tired and raspy; I thought with proper rest it would all clear up in time. When it didn't, I went back to the throat specialist who had examined me earlier; he had told me in no uncertain terms that I should not sing with laryngitis. Much to my disappointment, when he learned that I had not followed his advice, he left the examining room, absolutely refusing to help and take care of me.

At the end of that particular school year I had no prospects, options, or even one single idea as to how I was going to make a living with the music degree I was awarded. From the beginning, from my childhood, I had kept up with my musical studies just because I loved it, but now things were much different. I had to become fiscally self-sufficient.

Girls in the Middle East, especially in those days, were not brought up with the idea of a future goal or a career. To become professionals and achieve financial independence was not an option. Music and art were only to enhance the development of young women, as were embroidery and cooking.

I was not talented enough to become a concert pianist, and I knew it. However, I was more than willing to give keyboard instructions for a living. Then there was also singing. Perhaps I could also teach voice, but how and where does one start? To have a professional singing career was the farthest thing from my mind; besides, it would take no less than a genuine miracle to break into that profession.

As the school year was coming to an end, I was getting more and more desperate for a job; it was high time I started to make a living to support myself. My piano teacher, a lovely woman with whom I had studied for four years, had been planning to surprise me by giving me half of her students at the conservatory upon her semiretirement at the end of that year. Truly this was a generous gift to help start my teaching career, and right at the conservatory. I was deeply moved. But that was not to be.

In the meantime, thinking that with plenty of rest my voice would be okay, I had already contacted my closest classmate Lily in New York, who was under contract with the Metropolitan Opera Company's Young Artists' Program; I had asked her to please find out if there were any openings in the company's chorus.

If accepted, that would provide me with year-round, full-time employment, putting an end to all of my monetary needs.

Had I known at that time that singing with laryngitis had damaged one of my vocal cords, which no amount of rest would restore, I would have never asked for the favor. Within a couple of weeks I learned that there was only one opening in the chorus for exactly my type of voice, and was advised to be in Boston in two days for the required, already scheduled audition. Mind-boggling!

> *Dear Lord, I truly need your help again. Thank you, for you are already mindful of it.*

Chapter Thirteen

Boston / Unforgettable Audition

I was facing the most challenging competition in my life; it was exciting and scary at the same time. Was I ready to venture into another new and totally unfamiliar territory to continue my life's journey? There was no doubt in my mind that should the Met sign me up with a contract, of all my past experiences this would be the one needed step forward toward the realization of my dreams.

But what if I failed in my audition again? Then what? This was the Metropolitan Opera, the one company with the highest of all standards. However, should I succeed and be given an agreement, there would be nothing else left to do but start a career at the very top. This would be a happening beyond my wildest dreams. Did I deserve this honor? What a prospect! Since I needed a job desperately I should at least try, shouldn't I? Could not sit and do nothing, could I?

As fantastic as this chance was, I still had to make sure that this opportunity presented to me was in God's plan for my life. Fearfully, I asked the Lord to give me the assurance that this was his doing; otherwise, he should firmly close the door to this unbelievable opportunity. My prayer was sincere, yet at the same time in the secret corners of my heart I was hoping for the contrary. I had worked long and hard for so many years, and now I felt prepared, ready, and capable of walking into it.

> *Dear Lord, you have directed me thus far. Please help me succeed; **that is, only if it is your will**.*

Since I knew I was not all-wise and could not see the future, in any given situation, even now, I asked God's leading; if things moved smoothly, that is, without any obstacles, in childlike faith I would accept them confidently as the Lord's leading and act on it! For me the opposite holds true as well.

Several chains of events that had preceded this event were undeniably amazing, as if they were all prearranged and coordinated. You would think that by then I would have learned and understood that the Lord works in mysterious ways to synchronize circumstances. No?

First and foremost was the timing of the audition; a week later might have been too late, for the position could have been filled. Just a month before this most important upcoming tryout in Boston, I had been invited to sing at a church banquet in Philadelphia. By then, again by providence, I had acquired a new Lebanese passport, and for no special reason, had requested and was easily granted multiple entry visas to the States. Therefore my passport and visa were valid and ready for travel.

The bus, the most economical way to get to Boston, was out of the question, which meant I had to fly in order to be there on the appointed day and hour for my audition; if not, my getting to Boston on time would have been simply impossible. I also believe that the small savings I had was still there in the bank for this very purpose. I withdrew the very last remaining dollar, closed my account, and bought my round-trip airfare.

The next day I was on my way to Boston with the remaining small amount of cash in my pocket. That was the last so-called wealth left to my name. At this point I had nothing to lose but everything to gain. Some khutzpah! Eh?

It is a short flight from Toronto to Boston. Instead of nerves, I felt happy and truly lighthearted. It seemed to me I was singing, in my heart, all the way. As the plane started to descend, still high in the air, the most indescribable feeling overtook me; it grew stronger and stronger as we were circling over Boston. Even before we touched ground, I knew in my soul, without a doubt, that I was going to move to New York very soon to fill the opening they had kept available just for me. This job was mine, and I knew it. Unbelievable!

> *Lord, I thank you for your reassurance before the fact.*

After checking into the hotel where most of the company had registered, I went to the designated room where the chorus master and his assistant who was to accompany me were holding the auditions. After the customary greetings, I promptly handed over the introductory letter from my teacher, and then was asked for the list of the arias I had prepared. I was ready and excited to perform three operatic renditions, one in each language: Italian, French, and German.

When I finished singing the first aria, I felt I had truly done quite well; however, I didn't hear or notice any reaction from either one of them. Then I was asked to sing my second selection. I had barely sung a couple of phrases when I overheard the chorus master talking, so I stopped singing; then I heard him say to the accompanist "We are wasting time."

My heart sank deep into the pit of my stomach. Here I was singing with all of my passion, desperately trying to do my very best. What did he mean, they were wasting time? This was a real nightmare.

Then, for the first time looking directly at me, he said, "Be in New York by the middle of May to start rehearsals for the summer and fall seasons. You will get paid from day one."

Here we go again; once more I could not believe what I was hearing, but this time it was all positive.

Usually, even after a successful audition, one is used to hearing: "Please don't call us, we will call you if we need you." But to be hired this way, right then and there? This was unheard of. I had not quite recovered from the unbelievable, immediate invitation to join the company, when the chorus master, obviously being impressed, picked up the phone and called one of the regular conductors of the Met. He asked the maestro to hear me sing that very afternoon. What a great privilege! This was just too much for my little heart to bear.

Then I had to remind myself of the assurance I had already received: While still in the air, before landing, didn't you know, definitely know in your heart, that this position was left open just for you? Then why are you so surprised? Oh you of little faith. I was on cloud nine for the next few hours.

> *Thank you, Lord; you come through for me again and again.*

That afternoon a tall gentleman approached me at the concierge's counter and called me by my name. When I asked how he knew I was the one he was looking for, he simply said, "You look like a singer." This kind man who had heard and conducted the best singers at the Met, after hearing just one of my arias, asked if a chorus agreement was all I wanted and offered me a young artist solo contract. Had I not been concerned about the condition of my voice, I might have accepted his offer immediately with great excitement.

But at that moment I was more than happy that my voice had lasted long enough without becoming raspy during my singing. I was convinced a solo contract was not the best thing for me at that time, so I told him that perhaps in a couple of years I would audition for him again, and then gladly would accept his generous offer. This indeed was a second booster to my self-image and confidence in less than a few hours.

The next day I returned to Toronto with a great sense of accomplishment and the assurance of a confirmed singing employment. I had to put my affairs in order and soon was to leave for New York.

My kind and generous cousin Albert, who was aware of my financial situation, asked to see me privately and offered me five hundred dollars in cash before I left home. He said, "No one goes to New York without money." I assured him I would not need it, and that I was getting paid from the very first week. But that didn't matter to Albert. So I promised to repay him as soon as I got my first check. His response? "No need to rush."

How blessed I was to have had him and his wife as my surrogate parents for five years when I needed them most. Their kindness and generosity are seldom found anywhere. In turn God has blessed their whole family. My cousin is now a widower past his midnineties and still enjoys relatively good health.

A top designer by trade of fine jewelry for Birks of Canada and world renowned Cartier, Albert, a lifelong, self-taught scholar, daily researches the scriptures in their original languages, ancient Greek and Hebrew. Everyday he is up early writing booklets with a deeper perspective on biblical truths, for the edification and spiritual development of individuals who are interested in the Word.

He publishes and mails his works to many, near and far, with no cost to his readers. Today he lives with his daughter and son-in-law near his grandsons and great-grandchildren, respected and loved by the community. At his age he is still quite active, volunteering twice a week in two local old-age homes, visiting the sick and the aged, encouraging, praying and bringing to them the "Good News" of God's love. I hold him and his whole family in my heart now and always with deep love, respect, and gratitude. One meeting with Albert and you will agree that he is truly one of those most 'unforgettable characters'.

> *I thank you, Lord, for my cousins. Bless them continuously.*

Chapter Fourteen

Life in New York / Metropolitan Opera

Before I left Toronto, you can rest assured that I went to see the Director of the Canadian Opera Company in his offices. I needed to thank him, for I had learned a lot from him in four years of opera schooling. He congratulated me, also reiterating the importance and the honor of the position I was offered.

It was also time to visit the Director of the Royal Conservatory. The head of the school of music literally got up from his chair to hug me; it was obvious he couldn't be happier for me. Then with a twinkle in his eye, he said, "In the future, don't ever give up singing no matter who suggests it." We both knew that was an admission of the past fiasco.

The third stop in my rounds, and by far the most important one, was Dr. Walter at the university. I went to see him for the last time to pay my deep respects and show my profound appreciation for his generosity and kindness. I simply owed him *everything*: the successful completion of my education on gratis, and the regaining of my sense of self-worth and accomplishments.

And now, because of his direct and personal involvement in my special circumstances, he was also responsible for my full-time employment by the Metropolitan Opera Company, enabling me to become self-sufficient, independent, and ready to move on to a bright future.

Within a week or two after my successful audition, I moved to New York with my very few earthly personal possessions. The most logical place to check in without a two-year lease was the Young Women's Christian Association; that is until the company cleared my temporary residency status with the emigration office. After that I planned to find a conveniently located apartment of my own.

This was most gratifying; in my late twenties, finally for the first time in my life, I had become totally independent monetarily. I was no longer a student, no longer needing financial assistance either for schooling or for my living expenses. Becoming fiscally self-sufficient was emotionally liberating, the best medicine for my psyche and self-respect.

Once settled in, the first thing I did was to walk to the Lincoln Center to see the brand new, just completed

Metropolitan Opera House. It was 1966, the Grand Opening of the company's new home, and the beginning of my new career.

I'll let you imagine the feelings and thoughts that went through my mind as I walked in the plaza toward the front entrance of the world's most impressive, idolized company's new residence. I was well aware of the Metropolitan Opera's worldwide prestige, where throughout its long, magnificent history all the great international singers had performed. Now, only by the amazing grace of God, I was to be a tiny part of it. This was truly overwhelming.

Within a few days of my arrival, we, the company, left for Rhode Island where we were to give several open air summer evening concerts, and in the meantime started morning rehearsals on Benjamin Britten's Opera, *Peter Grimes*, for the upcoming season's premier in New York. Luckily for us, for a few hours each afternoon we became tourists, taking tours and visiting the famous mansions of Newport.

During our hotel registration I noticed another first year chorister, a contralto around my age; we were both novices and the youngest members of the chorus. We both looked somewhat ill at ease since neither of us knew a soul in the company; naturally we gravitated toward each other and decided to share our hotel accommodations for the rest of our stay.

Soon after settling in our room, Norma and I—for that was her name—discovered that we were both practicing Christians, sharing the same faith and values. Our personalities complemented each other, and so we became the best of friends. God in his wisdom had already provided me from day one a true, genuinely close friend, so I never felt lonely in this new phase of my life.

The summer months went by very fast. In the fall there was a tremendous excitement in the company. The new house was to open with pomp and circumstance. Marc Chagall's colossal murals, on either side and as high as the main front entrance of the building, were masterfully finished.

Samuel Barber, an American composer, was befittingly commissioned to write a new opera for the premiere performance, so he composed *Antony and Cleopatra*, based on Shakespeare's play, for the grand opening. Franco Zeffirelli, the great movie director, was the librettist as well as the stage director; plus Leontyne Price, whom I adored, was cast as the reigning star of the legendary evening.

The president of the United States, New York's governor and mayor, national and local officials, VIPs, and a long list of internationally known past and present opera singers were all invited to attend this unique and celebrated occasion. With their presence, they added an obvious opulence and excitement to that very special evening's performance, and later to the lavish festivities that followed, which lasted into the early hours of the morning.

For many to have given up the old, historic Opera House with its memories of great performers of generations past was indeed nostalgic, and yet to have built a brand new, beautiful House for the Performing Arts at Lincoln Center was indeed a monumental achievement.

The opening night was bursting with tremendous energy and great excitement, in the audience as well as behind the stage. It was curtain time. At a snail's pace the crystal chandeliers, a gift from the Austrian government, were gradually lifted up to the ceiling from their lowered positions. Finally it was time for the national anthem, in which the audience proudly and gladly participated.

With the opening bars of Barber's original score, to the unique sound of the Metropolitan's Orchestra and to the immense anticipation of the audience, the gold-colored, velvet curtain opened ever so slowly to the spectacular view of the elaborate sets and colorful costumes, not to the mention the magnificent sound of the first opening bars of music never heard before.

In the center of the stage was a turntable with a shimmering pyramid on it; live camels and goats were walking around; and we, the choristers, some in peasant and others in nobility costumes, moved among the spectacularly dressed soloists.

Such indescribable excitement; from the stage I saw a full house, four thousand people in standing ovation, and listened to their long, thunderous, spontaneous applause. The house was officially opened. My heart literally missed a beat; I needed someone to pinch me to bring me back to reality from my euphoric state. I kept repeating to myself, "Is this truly happening? Am I really standing on this very stage to perform?"

A few years before, when I took my first baby steps into my journey, it had never crossed my mind that one day I would be standing where I was at that moment. At the time an operatic career was the farthest thing from my mind; I had made no plans for this or any other professional career, neither had worked for it.

It seemed almost unfair compared to many who struggle to get where I was! This was a gift freely given to me on a silver platter; for what reason, I had no idea. Today a student, the next day I found myself on the Metropolitan Opera Stage! Miraculous! Unbelievable! It was at least improbable by any logic.

Somehow the busyness of my new daily life, the hard work, and the need to keep creative energies flowing never wore me down. Fortunately, from my childhood and throughout my student days, I had studied several foreign languages that were needed for opera; also, it was fortunate that I had already learned and performed more than half a dozen opera chorus parts, due to my three-year involvement in the Canadian Opera Company.

With all of that, I still had to memorize almost twenty new chorus parts in that first year alone. My daily schedule was heavy with several practice hours each and every morning, plus evening performances with two shows on Saturdays. Sunday was the day of rest, but only after morning church attendance. One could say I had a busy life!

Because of many more hours of daily singing than I was used to, in time my throat situation worsened, and I became further concerned with its condition. A few months after that unforgettable opening night, I went to see a throat specialist who gave me the devastating news: There was a polyp on one of my vocal cords, and no matter how long I rested my voice, this nodule was not going to melt and go away. It had to be removed surgically.

It was as if in that instant a light bulb turned on in my head. I knew without a doubt that this cyst had developed the previous year when in Toronto I was forced to sing with laryngitis. It was quite a scary time. Would I be able to sing after the operation? Would I lose my voice and my newfound job?

I went to the hospital by myself and checked in for the tricky procedure, trusting a doctor I had just met. Thank God, I was in the hands of a good surgeon and had great medical coverage with the Actors' Equity. I was also grateful to be working for a generous company such as the Met; no one made me feel guilty for having to keep absolutely mute for six consecutive weeks following my surgery, soon after they had hired me to sing. Sign language was the order of the day!

I was overjoyed and eager when finally I was permitted to talk and sing. Even after a successful surgery, totally healed, with a perfect pair of vocal cords, still psychologically I was somewhat apprehensive to use my full voice for fear of developing yet another nodule. I knew my vocal cords were now in good shape, yet something was not quite right with my singing; this was inexplicable, disturbing, and puzzling to me.

Somewhat concerned, not quite happy, and still slightly bothered by the way my throat behaved, I still kept on singing, rehearsing, and performing faithfully during the next three seasons. Each spring, I also toured with the company across the country, for six consecutive weeks singing nightly from our regular operatic repertoire. In those marvelous and exciting years I was a witness to and took part in some of the most unforgettable operatic performances with the best and the greatest leading, world-renowned singers of that day. Perfectly euphoric!

Please, Lord, even now, I need your complete healing.

Chapter Fifteen

Life Outside the Met

A year had gone by since my move to New York. I was still living at the YWCA where I had temporarily checked in upon arrival. I had not found or moved into my own apartment yet, simply because of the limited time I had for personal pursuits. One afternoon I came back from a very long day of rehearsals feeling quite tired and in need of a well-deserved rest. I had a couple of hours to put my feet up and relax. Later after a light supper I was to hurry back to the theater for that evening's performance.

As I was checking in, the desk clerk, who was a gentle and compassionate woman, mentioned that she had just registered another Armenian girl, who was also from overseas. Then, giving me her room number, she kindly suggested that perhaps I might want to give her a call since she was all alone in New York. Apparently this new young woman seemed exceedingly distressed, extremely anxious, and unhappy. When she was given the only room available with its bathroom facility down the hall, she became further disturbed.

I was truly exhausted when I got to my room. I lay down for a few minutes to relax, having made a solid promise to myself to call this new arrival at the "Y" the very next day. But my conscience would not let me rest; I knew firsthand what it was to be away from home, distressed and unhappy. I picked up the phone and dialed her room number; when she answered I introduced myself in Armenian, which gave her a new sense of hope and survival. I suggested we meet for dinner before I returned to work.

She was more than happy to meet with me in the dining room; that was the first of more than a few meals we had together. N'ver was a young woman born in Baghdad with a silver spoon in her mouth; her father was the dermatologist of the palace, to the then king of Iraq.

When younger, she was sent to Egypt for her education to the best available English school for girls at the time, and later to Switzerland to study the harp. From that point on her story had become deeply tragic; her depressed, sad expression was genuine and quite understandable. It seemed to me she had no enthusiasm or pleasure in life.

N'ver was made to come to the States by her parents in order to get her away from and forget her fiancé.

He was the one and only love of her life, but sadly, just before their wedding he was found to be terminally ill. So she was made to break their engagement, which in turn had broken her heart.

Soon after her arrival, she lost the one she had loved forever to the disease. She was crushed in spirit and all alone, had very few friends, and on top of it all, N'ver was having immigration problems.

There was not much I could do for her except be a compassionate listener, become a source of encouragement and a friend to her in her hour of need. For the next year or so we met occasionally for dinner; there was definitely a bond developing between us. We shared stories of our past life experiences and events, talking of our families and a variety of other subjects that two single women chat about when they get together.

Finally, after being stuck at the YWCA for two whole years, just before the beginning of my third season, I was delighted to find a studio apartment with reasonable rent that was within walking distance to the Met, and lucky for me, the unit came with a window air conditioner.

Immediately upon moving in I had my small, one-room flat carpeted: living room/bedroom, plus an entrance foyer which was also the kitchen. A sofa bed, a bookcase, and a small table, made to fit the tiny corner for dining with four chairs, that was the extent of my interior decor.

Two complete sets of towels, a set of four dishes and utensils completed my needs. I was fixing a home for myself, happy and excited to have my very own place for the first time in my life. Life was shaping up, and finally I was beginning to feel like a mature adult.

It was exactly twelve years since I had left home. All through those years, due to circumstances, I had remained a student, and had known very little in between but struggles. I had devoted my existence to full-time study and practice, and barely recovered from deep disappointments more than once.

In the four years in California I had moved four times, changed learning institutions, and then uprooted myself and moved to Canada. I lost two years of my education only to start all over again from the beginning. To top it all off, I also almost died tragically. But through it all, God had faithfully supplied ALL my needs in time, and at all times.

Now by the grace of God I had finally arrived at the threshold of a wonderful career and had a place that I could call home; yet through it all there was no one in particular that I could call my very own, my soul mate. Romance was not and had never been in the picture. Period!

Well-meaning friends would ask why a nice girl like me was still not married. To that I would jokingly respond: "What would you have me do? Stand in the corner of a street with a plaque hanging over my head, advertising that I am still single and looking for a husband?"

I must admit being single at times felt awkward and quite lonely, but I had no time to worry about it then. However, things were changing and were different now. I was finally settling into a life of my own, but still had no one to share my life's successes and failures, joys or sorrows with. All of my contemporaries were by now married and had settled down with their own families.

Through the years, individuals whom I found myself drawn to did not even know I was alive. With the same token, those who found me attractive, I had no feelings for.

> *Dear Lord, when? When will you provide that special right one, just for me?*

My dear friend Norma from the Met and I spent most afternoons between rehearsals and evening shows together; we often shared intimate, personal, as well as spiritual subjects. Her comment concerning my dissatisfaction with my single status was that I was at war with God, and that he would provide only when I stopped fighting him.

I disagreed, argued with her, and protested vehemently; I was not fighting . . . I was merely asking! "Asking," she would say, "is the same as questioning his wisdom, his will and plan for your life. It is a strong sign of lack of faith and a lack of complete trust in his promises, a symptom of being suspicious of his loving care and timing where your needs are concerned. You must stop asking and begin trusting."

Within a day or two after I had moved and settled into my one-room apartment, Norma's analysis clearly and forcefully came to the forefront and surfaced in my mind. Perhaps it was the total aloneness, the deafening quiet, or the absolute solitude that gradually but surely triggered a fierce, raging battle in my soul. I found myself wrestling with God in one-to-one combat.

I could not think of a good reason why he had chosen the single life for me so far, or possibly for always. I confessed that I did not know the answer to the "why" or the "when"; moreover, I was most unhappy with what seemed to me his total indifference, and in my discontentment I told him so.

After a long and painful struggle, amid unending strong arguments, I finally realized that each and every one of all my frustrations and resentments were being met solely with his patience, compassion, and gracious understanding. My warfare stopped, my will was broken; finally, humbly, I put down my weapons of discontent. The battle was won. I was defeated by his gentle love.

Then humbly I confessed to the One who had always loved me and provided for all my needs to date, that I did not understand, much less like my present, personal state, or his delay in being responsive to it; but that without reservation, I would submit to him and his plan for my life.

Right then and there, penitently, respectfully, and willingly I handed over my singleness to my Father in heaven. In thought and word I surrendered myself totally to his will.

It was then I offered the most difficult prayer of my life to date: *Farther, I am willing to accept anything from your hands that you deem best for my life, including remaining single without a love of my own, if that is what you have considered and chosen for me.* **Lord, not mine, but your will be done**".

In that very moment, miraculously my inner turmoil stopped abruptly and was replaced instantly with his comforting peace and a profound calmness in my soul. I learned a precious lesson that day: painful spiritual struggles of all kinds, meekly submitted to his will, are always followed by a quiet, serene, and deep spiritual tranquility and growth.

Oh, that we would be wise enough to put everything in God's hands sooner rather than later.

Chapter Sixteen

Beginning of a New Life

Within the second week after moving into my new, one-room living space, N'ver came over with a housewarming gift of ground Turkish coffee and two demitasses; we drank from the fresh brew to celebrate my newly found apartment. After a pleasant visit and with her many heartfelt good wishes she left; it felt great to have entertained my first guest.

I was somewhat surprised, however, when N'ver called me the very next day, so soon after our visit. She asked me if I remembered her mentioning, a year or so earlier, a young man from her family connections in Toledo. It is funny: I had no idea where Toledo was then.

I not only knew exactly who she was referring to, but I still could see the interesting expression on her face as she talked of him; it looked like she was mentally matchmaking. Well, she went on to say that he was and would be in New York for the next few days, and when she mentioned me to him in conversation, this gentleman was not only highly interested but quite insistent in wanting to meet and invite me out to lunch as soon as possible.

What? Was this a joke? Had I not made my peace with God just a few days earlier? Did I not agree that I was willing to remain single the rest of my life? And now, what was I to make of this? Besides, I did not believe in blind dates.

N'ver heard the hesitancy in my voice and tried to re-assure me that they were not only related but that she knew him quite well; if it were not so, she said, she would not have brought up the subject. While we were on the phone, I could hear music in the background, and I was curious to know where she was calling from.

Well, she was at the Pierre Hotel having lunch with the said gentleman; at his request the maître d' had brought the house phone to the table, and he had per-suaded her to call me right then and there.

I felt terribly uneasy having him sitting there and overhearing our conversation, so I asked her to please hang up and if she would like, we could talk about it the next day. N'ver was a very sensitive woman; I did not want to hurt her feelings, so later, after much hesita-tion and deliberation, also getting the opinion of other friends, finally I agreed to meet with him providing she, N'ver, would come with us to the luncheon. **Well, that was not acceptable to him and was not to be.**

The fact that this young man was not from New York and would soon be leaving somehow made my decision easier. Because of it, I felt sure that, just like my past experiences, this too was going to be a short "Hello" and "Good-bye" meeting anyway.

How little I knew that from the very beginning it was in God's plan to have the two of us meet when the time was right. He had kept not only myself, but him as well, single for all the past thirty plus years to bring us together precisely at the correct moment in our respective lives. Later the realization of this fact confirmed my walk of faith with God. He not only plans and executes, but when we get out of his way, he is willing and able to do all things perfectly and in the most fantastic way.

It is interesting how we can be impressed either positively or negatively by hearing just a few things concerning a stranger. Before I met Ed, I learned from N'ver that since his graduation from university, he had taught school and was a world traveler, a man quite sensitive to others' cultures, backgrounds, and their sensibilities. He passionately enjoyed classical concerts, operas, ballets, museums, art galleries, and lectures; for me these were all very desirable qualities in a man.

I met him that weekend; one had to be totally blind not to perceive within a few short hours that he was also a kindhearted, generous, gentle gentleman. Most importantly and above all else, he was a man who possessed a pure heart, a man with no guile in his soul.

My first awareness of Ed's sensitive and thoughtful nature was even before we met. I learned of his suggestion that since I was raised overseas and not quite accustomed to the American ways, he had thought in order to make me feel more comfortable perhaps N'ver should do the formal, in person, introductions before our date. That truly did not matter and was not necessary; I had been in this country long enough not to be bothered with such things; however, the fact that he was considerate of it meant a lot. **This was the first plus!**

When I was growing up in a different time and place, just as other young girls, I too was reminded often by older women to ask God's direction and his provision for a suitable mate. I remember even at twelve, before leaving home, I had started praying for a suitable future life partner, one who would possess a good and a clean heart. Money, good looks, popularity, or an influential individual was not even a consideration. At our very first meeting, it already became quite clear that this total stranger, Ed, was a man with a pure heart, which fulfilled my most important requirement in a man. **This was the second plus!**

From the moment of our first hello, driving down to the restaurant in a cab, he seemed totally relaxed; but the fact that I too was quite at ease with him, a total stranger, was extraordinarily unusual behavior on my part. It felt as if we had known each other in a distant past and were getting reacquainted. He had already made reservations at a certain Armenian restaurant for a Shish Kebab luncheon, and yet was willing to change his choice if I favored some other eating establishment. It was refreshing to meet a man who was mature enough to know what he wanted, and yet was flexible enough to accommodate someone else's preference. **And that was the third plus!**

Our conversation at the table was extremely easy, enjoyable, relaxed, and totally void of all innuendoes, and yet I was repeatedly thinking to myself that either he was totally out of his mind, simply crazy, or I was utterly absurd, positively ridiculous to think that he was in love with me. He had said or done nothing to arouse my suspicions or make me feel the way I did; still something in his eyes, unbeknownst to him, was betraying his true feelings. How could this be? Besides blind dates, I also did not believe in love at first sight.

I found this young man called Ed to be self-confident and yet not arrogant, strong but yet gentle, an intellectual, sensitive and kind. His international travels and worldview, plus his deep understanding and appreciation of life and people, had made him well-rounded and multidimensional. Those were traits I had always held in high regard; I esteemed them most desirable qualities in a man.

Later, in order to elongate our date, he requested we walk back to my apartment. That was from Twenty-eighth Street and Second Avenue, the east side of the city, to Seventy-fifth Street on the west side of Broadway: almost fifty blocks long and practically the whole width of Manhattan, which necessitated a short rest at the Waldorf Astoria on the way. During that very, very long walk, I knew in my heart that this casual meeting, as far as he was concerned, had already the definite beginnings of a serious relationship.

His sincere desire to familiarize himself with me was captivating and extremely flattering, yet at the same time terrifying. I strongly suspected and felt that very soon, there would be impending serious decisions that I had to make. I knew in my heart Ed was indirectly hinting at marriage, but how could this be? We had met just a few hours earlier. It was not possible; he simply could not be in love with me.

By the time he brought me home, I was convinced of his deep sentiments; it had become quite obvious, for he told me in plain language before we got to my apartment that he definitely needed to see me every day while in New York, for the next five days.

As for me, that year's operatic season had just ended. I had no more rehearsals or performances and soon was to leave for Montréal for my regular summer vacation. However, as providence would have it, the morning before our scheduled luncheon I had called the repair shop to find out when I could come to pick up my suitcases they were repairing.

I was told they had been extremely busy and therefore needed at least another five days to finish the job.

Because of it I had to delay my departure and remain in New York, for the next five days.

What? Was this a coincidence, or a divine plan?

Dear Lord, what now? Are you manipulating the dates?

Chapter Seventeen

Budding Romance

I found Ed to be very pleasant and a good conversationalist. His genuine curiosity in me was surely intriguing. For the next few days I actually had nothing else to do but wait for my suitcases to be fixed, so I had no excuses not to see him; besides, I was also curious to find out more about him. Did he come into my life in passing, or would he stay for life? Who was this man I found so charming? Besides, he was quite pleasant to be with, so I agreed to spend my time with him.

Before our first date was over, Ed told me that in three weeks, upon my return from Montréal, he was coming back to New York. He had already made plans to rent a furnished apartment, and would stay in Manhattan till fall; he wanted to get to know me and give me a longer time to know him better as well.

This was the first time in my life that someone was pursuing me earnestly and passionately with the most honorable of intentions. Why was he so strongly attracted to me? I was neither tall, slim, nor beautiful. *Remember?* My early childhood insecurities surfaced.

Those became the most memorable, singularly unusual days that I ever spent in quality time with someone who found me valuable enough to want to spend all his vacation time with me. It was also amazing, totally out of the ordinary, that for the first time I could remember, I had nothing to study, rehearse, or perform; therefore I had ample time to enjoy the attention of a good man.

Ed was there with me almost constantly throughout those infamous five days, except for the very next day when I was totally involved with my aunt who had just flowing in from Cairo. So in order not to miss a day, Ed was at my door at ten o'clock that same night, to take me for a midnight snack at a Jewish deli.

We sat there until past two o'clock in the morning talking, with the purpose of getting to learn more about each other. He was easy, relaxed, and most enjoyable to be with. The next few days we took leisurely walks in the city. Ed treated me daily to wonderful restaurants, making me feel very special, a woman without whom he could not live.

We spent those five days and evenings talking incessantly with the purpose of getting to know each other on as many levels as possible. For once, I felt like a woman who was one-of-a-kind to a very exceptional man. Besides treating me to fine restaurants, Ed also took me to different museums and art galleries; one rainy evening we even ventured to an open-air Shakespearian play in Central Park.

The last night we had together, Ed took me to an elegant Italian restaurant in Lincoln Center, and then to a performance by the Rome Opera Company. Afterwards we sat in the open-air café in front of the New York Philharmonic Concert Hall for more conversation over pastry and espresso.

Before we parted we exchanged phone numbers; Ed promised to write and keep in touch. The evening was a perfect ending to our five-day marathon of "getting to know you," which seemed full of promises to be only the beginning of a long and lovely relationship.

When we left New York and went our separate ways, it was July fourth weekend. I got to Montréal almost a week later than expected, and had to explain to my family about the unavoidable circumstances with my suitcases and meeting Ed. Naturally there was great curiosity about him from all.

I had time now without distractions to quietly and calmly pray, meditate, and examine my thoughts and feelings. I could feel the invisible, solid wall I had built long ago around my emotions for self-protection from possible hurt, was beginning to weaken and crumble, for Ed had begun gaining my trust.

Understandably, there were many valid questions that were constantly preoccupying my mind. Was it possible I was feeling something special for Ed only in response to his sincere affection for me? Or was I simply missing the special personal and constant attention I was getting from him? I was already thirty, and that was a sign of an old maid in the culture I was brought up in. Perhaps I was; or was I now more fearful of the loud ticking of my biological clock? Was I allowing myself to be drawn to Ed because I was lonely and had been for a long time? If I married him, would it last for a lifetime? Was this what *I* wanted or was our meeting the Lord's will and choosing for my life? Didn't I just give up the fight and make peace with God about my singleness? Even so, in the meantime I was willing to accept *whatever* he chose for my future, single or otherwise. Wasn't it I who at last prayed, "Your will be done"?

*Please, Lord, HELP! Direct my thoughts and feelings; show me **your will**.*

My mind was running in circles; then I remembered the words of my dear friend Norma from the Met: "When you stop questioning, that is, stop fighting God, that's when he can and will work on your behalf." Wow! Was this what was happening? I had just stopped fighting him. Could our meeting be actually his doing?

During my vacation there was a mail strike in Canada. So, no written word from Edward! And no phone calls either. For almost three weeks there was no word from the man whom I had met under unusual circumstances. He had given me clear and definite signals of his deep affection, subtly hinting several times of love and a lifelong commitment. This was not like him. I became especially concerned when I heard on the national news that more than two hundred people had died on US highways over the July fourth holiday.

Ed was driving from New York to Ohio all alone that very weekend; I was further disturbed when my person-to-person calls made clear that he was not home. I never found out if he was not at home that particular evening, or had not yet arrived in Toledo. After a week or ten days of waiting and hoping to hear from him, for my own sanity I began to think that he must be having second thoughts, regretting to have made a commitment so soon. Too soon!

At the end of my vacation, just the day before I left for New York, the mail strike was over and so I received a most generic postcard which Ed had mailed the day he got home. The card simply said that the weather was hot and announced his safe arrival. By then I had already begun thinking I should add my experience with him to the past list of unfruitful liaisons.

Thank you, Lord; at least he is okay.

Without a doubt our meeting had been quite similar to a whirlwind that threw me for a loop; most assuredly he had fallen in love with me at first sight, even before we had said hello. Those five days were like cramming for a life-altering exam: learn as much you can, as fast you can.

Though I had enjoyed his company immensely, yet I was not quite as ready to make a commitment as he was; so the anxiety I felt was obvious to both of us. For fear of seriously scaring me away, he had decided, while I was at home, not to press me further, allowing me time and space to help me find my bearings.

During those weeks in Montréal it never crossed my mind that Ed, who was a very sensitive man, might have realized that because of his own strong belief and conviction in our future together, he had emotionally pushed me, in that very short time, simply too far and too fast. So he had decided to let me be for a short while.

When I became aware of the depth of his understanding toward me, I was convinced that here was a prudent and a wise man. He not only knew himself well, but was fully aware, thoughtful, and considerate of someone else's state of mind and feelings.

But Lord, don't you think it would have been reassuring had he called me at least once?

Chapter Eighteen

Back in New York

When my three weeks were up, I returned to my apartment, and before I could close the front door behind me, the phone was ringing. To my pleasant surprise, Ed was on the phone. He was calling to let me know he was returning to New York that weekend as planned. It was refreshing to hear his voice again after several weeks of no contact. I was eager for his return in a curious way, and felt something special for him. Yet I was hesitant to admit it, even to myself. Yes?

Sure enough, in a couple of days Ed was back with the same and perhaps with even more enthusiasm over our reunion. I was glad to see him pull up in a cab on time, and when I opened the front door he embraced me affectionately. To my astonishment I responded quite naturally and warmly in kind. I knew in my heart I had missed him.

It was only befitting that when he returned, in order to reciprocate for the elegant restaurants and superb meals he had treated me to, for our first meal I needed to prepare a nice dinner for us in my new apartment. So I planned carefully and cooked a special meal, setting the table for two as nicely as I could for his first evening in New York.

During our meal, which consisted of Armenian rice pilaf and stuffed eggplants, first he did not recognize and then could not believe he was eating eggplants. Later he was amazed that his strong distaste for eggplants had suddenly disappeared. Was this my superb cooking, or was he, as his father later suggested, in love, and had no idea what he was eating?

We were having a pleasant time and enjoying just being together again; then quite unexpectedly, as if it came from nowhere in the middle of our meal and conversation, suddenly Ed brought me to tears in great panic. I heard him quite decisively and clearly tell me in detail all the plans he had already made for us.

It was WHEN, not IF we marry, we will have our wedding at the church in Montréal; later we will have the reception in the church hall. Then we shall go for our honeymoon to the Laurentian Mountains, just north of Montréal in Quebec.

He will move to New York and find a teaching position in Manhattan, or if need be, he will commute daily to a school in New Jersey; that is, if I choose to continue with my career. Otherwise he knows a couple of perfect places in Toledo for our first home.

I was plenty aware of his deep affection for me and was beginning to feel warmly toward him, but I hardly knew him long enough to marry him. It was wonderful to have him as a friend with perhaps future possibilities, but to have definite plans made for marriage after just five days, followed by three weeks of no communication? Besides, this was no proposal.

When he ended up telling me in great detail and confidence that I would see all the plans he had made for us come to pass before long, distraught, I literally broke down. Nervous, anxious, and confused, I wanted to know if he was in his right mind.

This was the perfect time and place to hear *Rodgers and Hart's* famous work in the background: "I'm wild again, beguiled again, a simpering, whimpering child again. Bewitched, bothered and bewildered—am I."

In my upbringing it was customary that the families would get acquainted with each other socially first, then we who were to be engaged would get to know each other on a personal level at least for a year or two before a serious step like marriage was even considered or discussed. His cute response? "I don't have that kind of time!"

At this we both laughed out loud. Then realizing that he had genuinely scared me and caught me totally off guard, he calmly and with great conviction tried to reassure me that he knew and was sure beyond a doubt that everything he had envisioned for us will come true. I asked him how he could be so sure of this, especially when in truth he had had very little time to get to know me. At that, he pointed to his heart and said, "Something in here told me so."

Then I suspected he must have experienced what I too have known firsthand: a sense of knowledge. It was as if he had been given a vision. This was serious stuff!

For the next three weeks all I had was several open air evening concerts in Central Park, so we had the luxury of spending all of our days together. Ed and I made the tour of other gourmet restaurants; he introduced me, among others, to Japanese, Russian, and Hungarian delicacies. We attended a meeting at the United Nations, took a boat ride all around Manhattan, and still there were more museums and galleries to visit.

Once we took a romantic horse-and-buggy ride in Central Park, which clearly reminded me of my early childhood: often we used the same old-fashioned way to go to church on Sunday mornings, since besides the streetcars that was the only other mode of transportation available in those days.

One day Ed as usual hailed down a taxi, he needed to take me somewhere in preparation for the future. I could not believe it when forty minutes later I realized we were still in the cab going to Long Island. "This area is reminiscent of Toledo," he said "I wanted you to see it." So finally he asked the cab driver to drop us at the next corner, from where it was only a couple of blocks to the French restaurant (he said in error). He had been there in the past and was sure I would love their food. We did not have to go that far for French food. But Ed's real intention was for me to leisurely walk a short distance and observe the neighborhood, to get an idea as to what Toledo looked like.

After more than thirty-five blocks of walking and many blisters later—which my new shoes had rewarded me with—we got to the restaurant only to find it closed for the month. It was their summer vacation.

By then I was limping in pain with my bandaged, sore feet. So Ed called another cab to get us to a near-by Italian restaurant instead. The driver chuckled: the bistro was at the end of the same block; no need for him to drive. I remember Ed asked to him to drive on anyway, since his companion was not capable of taking another step. We had a fantastic meal at that typical Italian restaurant with its red-checkered table-cloths, and to the spirited singing of operatic arias by the waiters as they served.

You can be sure I insisted on taking the subway back from Long Island to Manhattan. Unbelievably, he had taken me all that distance in a cab, just to have me feel good about moving to Toledo. Ed was unusual in so many ways; life was never boring with him.

Throughout and in between all these outings, our lengthy conversations were unending; we shared openly our convictions on every subject imaginable:

religious, social, political, and monetary, discussing our likes and dislikes, personality traits and idiosyncrasies.

We kept sex out of our relationship, but the very personal questions—and there were many—I needed to know the answers of; they were extremely important to me. I had to know and be thoroughly known by this total stranger if I were to wed him. In turn I was as honest as I could be with him concerning myself.

Ed was very mature and free of hang-ups; he knew himself quite well and was like an open book. I found all his answers extremely honest and in earnest. Incredibly, much to my astonishment, he took time to tell me of all his shortcomings and personality quirks. This was so very unusual and refreshing, it made me think: "This man is too good to be true. Is he for real?"

Dear Lord, is there someone left in this world as wonderful as my father?

Chapter Nineteen

Crisis Resolved

At the end of the second week of his stay in New York, one unforgettable afternoon our liaison reached a critical peak; it was only after the storm had subsided that I knew for sure I had turned an important corner in our relationship. It was as if that day, Ed cracked open the protective shield I had built around myself and broke down my defenses.

I got dressed up for a very special date as he had wished; he was to take me to a classy place for our romantic rendezvous. We were both elegantly attired: he in his dark suit, I in my white, three-piece knitted ensemble, and to complete the look, a large, wide-brimmed white hat.

The funny thing was that instead of the usual cab ride, upon his request we walked block after block, I in my high-heeled, white shoes, on sidewalks that were wet from the washing of the bloody floors of a fish market, banana peels from fruit stands, and other piled up dirt.

We were on our way to the Plaza, one of the most elegant hotels in those days, for their afternoon high tea served with dainty cucumber sandwiches, petit fours, and other delicacies. Appropriately, Ed asked to be seated in a secluded and quiet corner.

Soon after we had ordered, my romantic, eager friend wanted to know how close I had come to feeling love for him. We both knew I was quite fond of him, but love him? I reminded him that he was not supposed to pressure me but was to give me willingly all the time I needed.

However, now he was pressing me for an answer. I truly, genuinely, and deeply liked him, felt a great admiration for him, enjoyed his company always, and was incredibly comfortable with him, but was not sure that I loved him.

As he pressed me for an answer and a commitment, to his dismay I could not tell him what he wanted to hear. Instead, he found me intensely troubled and in tears once again. I, on the other hand, was desperately attempting to hide my face from other patrons under my big, wide, picture hat.

Fearing he was deeply distressing me, extremely disappointed and profoundly frustrated, Ed seriously suggested returning to Toledo the very next day. To me that made no sense either; he had already paid in advance for his furnished apartment for a third week, still he wanted to cut his stay in New York short. Yet that was exactly what I needed: more time.

Ed became acutely aware of my deep distress. The next thing I knew, within minutes he was motioning for the maître d' and explained that he wanted a phone. (I was well-acquainted with his "must have a telephone" in restaurants during important situations.)

He explained that he wanted to call his school superintendent and request a leave of absence for a year from school. Just like that! With a drop of a hat! He decided right then and there, making a complete about-face, that instead of leaving the next day, he was going to move to New York and find a teaching position either in the city or New Jersey for the next school calendar. If what I needed was more time with him, he was ready to give me a whole year.

I knew that Ed was quite secure in his school system since he had been awarded tenure; he liked and was liked in a special way by the administration and colleagues alike. Besides, his idea was quite risky: after a year of absence there would be no guarantees; he could lose his position permanently. I could not let him do this in good conscience; I was not about to gamble with his life. So after I reassured him that he was not going to lose me, I insisted he return home when the time came.

After he calmed down, I explained to Ed that if I couldn't know for sure that I was in love with him after three weeks of open daily communication, and all that we had truthfully shared, what made him think that while he was away, I could fall in love overnight with someone else?

All I needed was to be sure, very sure, that what I felt for him was genuinely true love. The reassurance I gave him seemed to give him the serenity he needed. He no longer needed the phone.

This, his sacrificial gesture, his willingness to move and spend a whole year in New York, made me realize fully how profound and intense his love was for me. He was willing to risk his future security in order to win me over. No one had ever cared for me like that before. How could anyone not respond in kind to a love that is so pure and selfless?

At the end of the third week, the last morning of Ed's stay in New York was also the first day of my rehearsals for the new season. We had breakfast on Broadway right across from the Lincoln Plaza with my friend Lily. Later he called a cab for the airport, then right there on the sidewalk in clear daylight with people watching, he kissed me, sat in the taxi, and from the open window said to me, "I know that I love you. You will find out that you love me too, sooner than you think."

Before I could recover my composure and regain my senses to at least respond with a good-bye, the cab quickly whisked him away. Definitely Ed's final words left me dumbfounded and speechless. I asked, "What just happened?" Lily had to repeat his parting pronouncement, word for word.

Lord, what am I to do now? I am scared and confused. Please help me.

Chapter Twenty

Empty, Lonely Manhattan

It was a short walk from the restaurant across and through the Lincoln Plaza to the theater. My friend went directly to her appointment and I, thunderstruck, with Ed's parting words still ringing in my ears, dragged myself further through several corridors to the choristers' practice hall.

I was secretly overjoyed, actually thrilled, when before the rehearsal began I was among several of us singers who were unexpectedly excused from that morning's and the rest of the week's scheduled rehearsals, which also meant, from all of the performances of *Boris Godunov* throughout the year. That was to guarantee us a free night periodically during the season.

The reason for my immense relief was simple; my mind was in total disarray, and my soul was in deep turmoil after the emotional cyclone Ed had put me through for three consecutive weeks. Though I had been intensely bothered by my lonely life, when Ed came into my clearly defined, organized, structured, and finally somewhat successfully settled life, he had overloaded me with serious considerations concerning my future. They were all coming at me at a high speed and seemed to be immediately around the corner.

It would have been impossible for me in my frame of mind at that time to concentrate, learn, and memorize adequately a new repertoire, particularly in Russian.

Upon our dismissal I gladly left the theater, going directly to my little apartment for the quiet and the privacy I needed; I required a peaceful place to think things over.

No sooner had I gotten home when unexpectedly a sense of deep loneliness engulfed me. I felt abandoned and all alone with nothing to do, nowhere to go, and no one to talk to for the day and the following week. The silence in my little home was deafening. Ed, who had kept me busy every moment of every day during my vacation, was gone; there were at least nine to ten million people in New York City at that time, but I still felt lonely and lost.

The quiet and privacy I thought I needed were not helpful; instead, a strong desire to go home gripped me. The next morning I was on my way to Montréal. Perhaps to be with my family would help fill the agonizing void I felt; at least I could vent my thoughts and feelings and share them with my loved ones.

All during my trip I prayed that the Lord would give me wisdom in my choices and clear my mind from its turmoil. I was facing the most important decision of my life, and I needed help; there were plenty of unanswered questions that were crisscrossing and spinning with a fast pace in my head at the same time.

Perhaps my dear mother, who was much more pragmatic than I, was the one I should talk to. At times I found her rather amusing with her logical, common-sense approaches, responses, and solutions. This is how my conversation went with my mother.

"Ma, I am so confused; I don't know if I really love him."

"For someone whom you say you don't know if you love or not, why are you thinking of him every moment?"

"But, Mother, I am facing the most important decision of my life. Of course I am thinking . . ."

She looked at me through the top of her glasses, stopped crocheting for a moment to respond to my next question.

"Mother, how did you know Father was the one for you when you married him?"

"Ohhhh, you are asking silly questions. In those days there was no 'I love you, do you love me?' It was all arranged marriages. Later I did love your father, and you know how much he loves me too."

At that we both giggled like two school friends.

I knew exactly where she was coming from; my mother was realistic and practical in her thought processes. I figured that emotionally there would be little help from her. But then, truthfully, who can really help anyone in such a personal choice?

I resorted back to my private talks with the Lord. In the past I had always relied on that certain feeling of peace, calmness of soul and spirit, that to me was a sure sign of his direction and will in any and all of my decisions. Prayerfully I was hoping and waiting just for that!

After several days of constant prayer and meditation, during one of my conversations with the One from whom all love, grace, and blessings flow, my mental and emotional turmoil incredibly, instantly, vanished.

No more doubts or fears, no more unending questions. Instead, there was again that same, familiar, clear, peaceful, and unmistakable sense of knowledge concerning the path I was to take.

My mental unrest was gone; it was replaced with a gentle serenity. I knew for sure that from the very beginning, God was orchestrating the details of my life for this very moment in time. At every step and turn in my journey, up the hills and down in deep, dark valleys, without fail, he had sent his angels in human form to help, guide, and give me the strength and courage to go on, to get me to this point in my life's journey.

It was then and only then that I knew in my heart our meeting was undeniably from God. Finally, I was sure beyond any doubt or reservation that the strong affection I felt for Ed was unquestionably, unadulterated true love, and that, was from God too.

I could see clearly now the chain of events from my youth, how with a clear vision and deep conviction, I was made to feel strongly that *I had to leave home.* All the preliminary preparations for my departure were accomplished without a hitch, and in the nick of time I left for California.

A few years later different events forced me, and by faith I moved and settled in Canada. It had to be only from Toronto, not Montréal, San Francisco, or anywhere else that the door to my future miraculously could and did open, which led me back to the States, but this time to New York City, where I had to be to finally begin my professional singing career.

There in New York, due to circumstances beyond my control, I got stuck for two years at the YWCA, which turned out to be a blessing in disguise. There I met N'ver, and through her I was introduced to Ed, he who was to become my soul mate and the fulfillment of my true destiny.

What extensive, interwoven situations! Only he, the Lord, could have coordinated each and every one of them, and brought all into fruition in time to bless my life, and bless he did so very abundantly.

Father, you have been quite busy on my behalf guiding my life. I thank you for your constant, loving care.

In all honesty, in the three weeks Ed and I had spent together, after literally and thoroughly scrutinizing him, I had not been able to find one reason to reject him or his love. Besides loving me, his personality fitted mine like a kid glove and made me feel whole. He was the balm for my long-held emotional scars.

For the first time in my life I was looking and seeing myself closely though his eyes; moreover, I liked what I saw. He simply made me feel good about myself, inspiring self-confidence, the kind I never knew before.

I was convinced that Ed loved me with his whole heart, which he demonstrated in many ways. The most undeniable proof of his love for me was not only his constant, unwavering devotion, but his dramatic gesture and the generosity of his spirit; I could not forget the way he risked his whole future in order to win me over. If that was not true love, what is? This man was indeed in love with me, and in my heart I was surely responding to his love.

Interestingly, I knew I loved him too, sooner than I thought. I could almost hear him, self-confident and with unmistakable conviction in his parting words: "I know that I love you. You will find out that you love me too, sooner than you think."

So his prediction came true. Within two weeks of his pronouncement, I did write him a one-liner: "I think the answer to your question is 'Yes.'"

Of course he never *asked*, but simply *told* me, "*When we marry* . . . etc . . . etc . . ." However, I must admit, when I finally reminded him of it five years into our marriage, he did me the great honor of coming down on his knees where he then formally, properly proposed.

Lord, I thank you for Ed's unwavering persistence in pursuing me.

Chapter Twenty-One

Back To New York

I returned to New York a changed person. Instead of fear and confusion, there was a guarded excitement in me. However, our courtship had developed at such a fast pace that I was beginning to think this was all but a beautiful dream. I needed to make sure he was real and not a phantom.

Thinking of Ed, I could see all his facial features separately, but was not able to put them together. I simply could not remember his face. Panic hit.

Besides being convinced that I must have completely lost my mind, I was not sure how Ed would react if he knew the kind of tricks my crazy mind was playing on my emotions now. Instead, immediately upon getting my urgent, simply titled SOS note, he called to say he was flying back to New York for that weekend. Friday evening when I opened the door, he was standing there with open arms and a big, warm, disarming smile. "Remember me?" he asked.

We were both in our early thirties and facing life anew; this time not as individuals, but as one. We spent that short time together like two kids excited over their Christmas presents; we were eagerly planning our immediate future *together*. That was a new and exhilarating experience for both of us.

That weekend went by rather quickly; we were already looking forward to our next get-together. Ed was to return in three weeks so we could fly together to Montréal for my youngest sister's wedding. He had very much wanted to meet my family, and here was the perfect opportunity. By now my family was also more than curious to meet him; he was to be the fifth and the last son-in-law. What a uniquely fascinating meeting that promised to be for us all.

Ed came back to New York as planned and we flew together to Canada. There was not much time between our arrival and the scheduled wedding ceremony. Fortunately, the wind seemed to be moving in the correct direction, for we landed, thankfully, earlier than expected.

We got to the church just seconds before my father began walking down the aisle with my baby sister. As they entered the church, I was to sing the Lord's Prayer. Believe me, keeping my tears back and my emotions in check while I sang was not easy.

Later, it took me an extra few minutes to wipe off my stage makeup, which I still had on since I ran out of the theater to make it to the airport on time. So I was slightly delayed going down to the church hall for the reception; by then my dear, sweet, newfound friend, who knew practically no one in Montréal but still felt very much at home, was already there congratulating all who were in the receiving line and beyond.

I overheard him introducing himself as my fiancé, and without being prompted, he was also telling everyone loud and clear, "Yes, I know! I am getting a wonderful girl."

After all, this was the question he was always asked in New York from all my friends: "Do you know? You are getting a wonderful girl." He knew instinctively he was going to be asked the same question again and over again; so in his funny way he was saving them all the trouble, assuring them that he already knows he is "getting a wonderful girl."

During the festivities my father announced our formal engagement, of which most of the guests were already aware. Later at home we ordered my engagement and our wedding rings from our cousin Albert. As soon as they met him, my whole family embraced Ed as part of our family. Reality was truly and finally settling in!

The next day we flew back to our separate destinations. The following month was my turn to meet Ed's family. I flew to Ohio and met Ed's father, brother, his wife, and their children. His whole family accepted and was wonderful to me from day one. It was such a blessing to have both our families welcoming us with open arms. All were genuinely happy with our respective choices. Everything felt just right and all was well with the world.

I thank you, Lord, for our families and their love toward us.

I know we would have married soon after that, but I had already signed and had to honor my yearly contract with the Met. During that time we lived our lives looking forward to our periodic short visits and phone calls; in the meantime, we enriched the airline and phone companies. Ed still chuckles to this day when he talks of our long-distance courtship.

During that year, we would see each other or get together only eight times before our wedding day. Thanks to our endless sessions of open-wide communications, we had come to know each other as much as one can learn about and understand another human being; we had also become the best of friends.

There were no surprises, difficulties, or even uncomfortable adjustments that often happen in the beginning of many relationships and early married life. Soon it will be forty-five years since we first met. Love, joy, and respect intermingled with plenty of humor are still alive in our marriage, except today our feelings for each other run deeper and are truly unshakeable.

Most of our friends think that we must be working hard for the success we enjoy in our marital life; if we are working hard, we are not aware of it. When one loves and enjoys one's craft, practicing constantly and working with great dedication at it, is neither boring nor tiring; on the contrary, there is pleasure in the very process of it. At the end of that commitment one can hear or see and take pleasure in the beauty of their accomplishments.

I believe the very same principle is true in marriage. How can a relationship suffer or break apart. If both parties believe in loving and giving 100 percent of themselves for the well-being, joy, and fulfillment of their loved one 100 percent of the time, is that work or pleasure? Thank God we both believe that there is no room for selfishness in a marriage, and then there will be no room left also for failure

After serious considerations I had decided that following our wedding, which was only a few weeks after schools were out, I would move to Toledo. Remaining in New York would have meant that Ed had to teach in less desirable conditions, and perhaps commute long distances daily. Besides, his full-time teaching and my schedule of morning rehearsals plus evening performances would not have allowed much time for solid bonding in our marriage. To me that was the most important priority, so the choice was easy to make.

Ed did not want me to stop singing altogether, so we agreed that I would continue performing whenever I could find or create an opportunity to do so locally. That was quite acceptable to me, and I was content.

When the Lord changes the direction of our lives, every step forward becomes effortless with no complications. By early spring I had already transferred my apartment lease to a colleague, sold the few pieces of furniture I owned, packed the rest of my belongings, and had them shipped to Toledo.

Soon after that, I left New York for the last time to travel throughout the States with the company on the yearly scheduled spring tour. Ed was still teaching in Toledo, and I was on the road all over the country, yet we were confidently relaxed because at the same time, back in Montréal, our wedding and reception preparations were being successfully arranged by my older sister and her husband.

At the end of our tour, saying good-bye to my colleagues and friends was not easy; besides, the life I thought I was prepared for, worked long and hard for all those years, was being cut short. It seemed that God in his wisdom had chosen this temporary career to satisfy a sense of fulfillment in me, and in the meantime had successfully gotten me to New York, precisely where I had to be to meet Ed.

I finally realized that the purpose for the goings and comings, wanderings to and fro, and many travels on rough roads throughout my life was in order for me to arrive at my final destination of his choosing.

Now I knew beyond a shadow of a doubt that there always was a master plan in God's will for my life. He was from the very beginning leading, manipulating circumstances through successful or uncomfortable situations, to finally bring me to a place markedly better than what I could have imagined or asked for, where he had prepared a far more fulfilling life for me with the man I had fallen in love with.

At last, I was going to bask in total contentment with a strong sense of belonging, in my own love nest.

> *Thank you, Lord. Even now you close windows in order to open infinitely preferable doors.*

Chapter Twenty-Two

Our Wedding

It was early June when at the end of our tour, I left directly for Montréal. Several weeks earlier I had the necessary materials for my wedding dress sent over from New York. The off-white satin fabric enough for my gown, and its removable cathedral-length train I was to finish sewing, before carefully nestling into each French lace appliqué a small cluster of white pearls. I was looking forward with excitement to complete my work before Ed's arrival.

Out of necessity, throughout my young adult life I had always sewn my clothes, so I felt quite confident I was up to the task. The greater challenge was to design and create a head covering made of the same lace, and fasten it to a crown to complete my bridal ensemble. I was amused when unintentionally, but quite successfully, it ended up looking like a perfect duplicate of an old Egyptian pharaonic headpiece.

In one week, I had finished the gown to my immense satisfaction. School was out, and Ed arrived in Montréal just fifteen days before our wedding. Fortunately, all other necessary preparations were taken care of, so Ed and I could without delay go to the American Consulate to start working on my immigration file. Here we go all over again: Papers, Papers, Papers!

The act of completing official documents one more time, made me think of that great aria which Magda Sorel sings in Gian Carlo Menotti's opera *The Consul*. This was the plight of a poor, unfortunate woman who wanted to come to America, so she was asked to fill in paper after paper with unending questions.

For me to reenter the United States now meant I needed a visa that would identify me as a permanent resident, quite different than my student's or any other entry permit. So for the next two weeks, we spent many hours going back and forth to the US Consulate in preparation for my documentation. Once everything was put in order, from then on all I would need was my "Green Card" to be able go in and out of the country without any red tape.

Like a miracle, a copy of my lost birth certificate, the first requirement by the American Consul, arrived from Cairo the morning of our wedding; there could have been no greater bridal gift. Among other official papers, we needed documents to prove that I had never participated in any criminal activities, so police reports were required from every country I had lived in since my sixteenth birthday.

What a nightmare, I thought to myself! It might not be difficult to get reports from the States and Canada, but who could get a response from the Egyptian authorities? For sure to get the necessary affidavits would take a very long time, but they were absolutely imperative; without them I would be refused to re-enter the US with my new husband. Horrors! I knew we had to take care of those, but it had to be only after our honeymoon.

From the United States and Canada, immediate family members, relatives, and friends had already arrived a day before our wedding to celebrate, share, and join in our happiness on the most important day of our lives.

A few days before our marriage ceremony, I went to my father with all the love I could muster to have a heart-to-heart, private conversation with him. I would not and could not offend my dad for the world. I needed to know for certain that what I was about to ask would not hurt his feelings. My father's reaction was typical of him, generous in spirit and kind. "This is your day; anything you wish will be all right with me," he said.

I asked dad with utmost sensitivity if he would be terribly disappointed if at my wedding I chose to walk down the aisle alone, by myself, without him as my escort. I was most thankful that in actuality my father seemed openly relieved at my request. I still could remember, but would not remind him, of how emotional he became a year before, walking my youngest sister down the aisle.

After having gone over my big hurdle without breaking my father's heart, I then clarified the basis for my request to both of my parents. I believed strongly I was no longer that little girl who left the home-nest many years ago; now much older, at thirty-two, having lived away for so many years, I had become my own person. At my age, no one could truly give me away, but I, as a responsible adult, of my own free will, choose to come down the aisle and stand at the altar to give myself to the man I loved. This was the only non-conventional segment of our otherwise traditional wedding ceremony.

Long before the mid-afternoon wedding service had begun, from the balcony above, the organist was playing soft, appropriate music; the small, intimate chapel was made to look romantic with lit candles, and white rose petals were already strewn in the aisle in preparation for a bridal entrance.

My four sisters, starting from the eldest, walked down as bridesmaids to the altar before me. Following right behind them, I entered the church to a slow, passionate, operatic intermezzo. My bouquet with white roses and gardenias spread their perfume as I walked down the aisle.

At one point I looked up and saw Ed standing there at the altar, smiling, looking exceptionally handsome, his gentle, loving eyes fixed on me. I thought to myself:

"Here we go; this is it. This is the first day of the rest of our lives." *Please, dear Lord, bless our union.*

After a tastefully short and simple ceremony, on the way downstairs to the reception hall my poor mother had a dangerous fall, head down; it is a miracle she survived the accident. That created a big commotion during which one of my more sensitive sisters fainted from fear; in that upheaval, soon an ambulance arrived, and Mother was rushed to the hospital.

But, just like in the theater world, we figured "the show must go on." Even with deep concerns for the mother of the bride, we went on with the reception with my older sister standing in for her next to my father in the receiving line.

Later, with plenty of worry and uneasiness, we were all at home waiting for Mother's return from the emergency room. Finally around midnight, much to our relief and thankfulness, though in great pain, Mother was safely home, having survived what could have been a fatal fall. Well, you could say we had an unusually eventful day.

Exactly, to the last letter, as Ed had planned and announced to me a year before, we did get married in Montréal and honeymooned in the Laurentian Mountains of Quebec. It was a wonderfully intimate, quaint, French resort hotel; this was the ideal place for a getaway. We had gone through a whole year of several dramatic, life-altering situations, concerns, preparations, hectic schedules, travels, and adjustments.

The typically romantic, European looking inn was surrounded with beautifully manicured flower gardens; a picturesque small, private lake; cool, refreshing breezes; and a hotel that offered daily superb, continental cuisine. You can be sure we totally took advantage of the calm and peaceful atmosphere of the hotel; we thoroughly enjoyed the quiet relaxation they provided, which we had needed desperately for a long time.

Regretfully, our week of leisure and precious time alone together was over too soon; we drove several hours through lush green mountains, hills, and valleys back to Montréal. Returning from our honeymoon, we found my mother still in excruciating pain. She was recuperating from several broken bones in one of her arms, which was in a full cast from her fingers to her shoulder.

Friends and family members, just like in the old country, would come to visit unannounced all day long, some arriving at eight o'clock in the morning. They would call out from street level, three floors below, and then simply show up at our front door for morning coffee. They were there first to see how my mother was doing, and then wanted to have another chance to congratulate the bride and groom once again.

Ed thought this was hilariously funny. He would comment often, saying: "The Turkish coffee cups come, the Turkish cups go; then they come again only to go right back to the kitchen to be washed for the next arriving guests." Then I would add: "We need one maid in this house just to serve coffee."

We were to stay with my parents for the summer while working on completing my official papers at the American Consulate. We waited weeks for the required police reports from Egypt, California, New York, and Canada. Interestingly, the one from Egypt was the first to arrive, thanks to an uncle of mine who still lived in Cairo.

There was no problem hearing from the New York State Police Department as well as the Royal Canadian Mounted Police, but there was no word from Sacramento. I was told their offices were extremely disorganized, and not to be too surprised or disappointed if we did not hear from them at all. This was bad news!

The date of our return to the States was soon approaching. The consul told me that if my papers were not ready by then, Ed would have to go back, but I would have to stay behind until my file was completed. Bashfully I asked him if he could in good conscience do that heartless thing to a new bride.

Much to my relief, it turned out that he was joking. Then he reassured me that they would contact the FBI on my behalf, and if the FBI cleared me, I would be cleared indeed throughout the country, including California.

Besides solemnly swearing countless times to the truthfulness of my statements, and saying "I do" innumerable times, I also was fingerprinted scores of times, perhaps more than most criminals.

Today I have a spotless profile record throughout numerous countries, from Egypt's Police Department to the Canadian Royal Mounted Police and the offices of the FBI.

> *I thank you, Lord, for your ever-present help.*

Chapter Twenty-Three

Early Married Life

S ummer was ending; it was time to leave and head back to Toledo to set up house. This was literally going to be my very own first home to live in with the man I loved and married. Soon school reopened and Ed left every morning for early classes. I used to watch him drive away from a second-floor window, praying that God would be with him, protect him, and bring him home safely in the afternoon. I finally had found the love of my life, and I was afraid of losing him.

In that short time, my best friend had turned into my life partner and had already become so much a part of my essence, the center of my being, that it seemed my life actually began only after I met him. It was as if my previous existence, from childhood on to that day, with all of its experiences, was someone else's reality. I could not envision my present or future life without him. *My husband!*

Ed had strongly suggested that I do nothing stressful in our first year of marriage, no part-time job or even singing pursuits for a while for his new bride. I had studied, practiced, worked hard, and been on the go for thirteen consecutive years without a vacation. He recommended I have a long and complete rest; in other words, become- a lady of leisure. Deep down I could see the wisdom and the benefits of his advice, and so I was more than happy to comply.

It was fun to go together to buy new furnishings for our freshly painted apartment, part of the family-owned duplex. Besides the new paint job, Ed's father had also installed wall-to-wall carpeting for our whole apartment and purchased a new refrigerator that completed the kitchen. To crown off his wedding gifts, we were to live there with no rent for the first year. Ed's father was a kind and gentle soul. The fruit does not fall too far from its tree.

For the first few months of our marital bliss, I enjoyed spending time decorating our home, made draperies, refinished and reupholstered a few small old, pieces of furniture. After we were settled in, it was time to experiment with new recipes, which was another passion of mine. I dabbled again in oil painting and other hobbies I had always enjoyed.

Much later in our marriage, with Ed's inspiring encouragement I pursued several other interests of mine, including starting a small business which was short-lived; nevertheless, no amount of effort was wasted;

they all expanded my horizons. All these were price-less gifts! I enjoyed being alive and in love.

"Life is but a dream," goes the song; that surely held true in our case. We were living in Camelot. Many predicted that the euphoria we were experiencing would not last; we were warned that sooner or later we would have a rude awakening, find ourselves deeply disappointed in marriage and each other, and then that would become the order of the day. Well, that turned out to be a lie. After some forty-four years of happiness, I have no intention to start looking out for that day.

In those early years when tears would come . . . and they came often enough . . . much to Ed's immense relief he soon learned that, contrary to the past, those were now simply tears of joy. It took the poor fellow awhile to comprehend that tears are an unspoken affirmation of great contentment and the evidence of overflowing, profound bliss. My deep delight was in the knowledge that if and when the Lord builds the home, he secures it onto a firm foundation; therefore, it does and will stand solid for all time. Such security!

Before long my year of leisure was up. I was to find a vocal teacher / coach to work with. It was clear to me that I knew what to do technically, but my voice was unresponsive to it. If I could only with some help overcome this problem which was keeping me frustrated, everything would be all right with my singing. And so I thought. The truth be told, even though I found a teacher and started working with her, yet I was convinced that eventually it was up to me to discover and fix whatever the difficulty with my voice was.

Discontented with the little progress I was making, still for the next several years I gave a number of solo recitals at the Toledo Art Museum. It was there also that I performed with the Toledo Symphony Orchestra. One of the highlights and the most spiritually satisfying of all my performances was a little gem of a Christmas opera by Gian Carlo Menotti, *Amahl and the Night Visitors*. A few years later I had the privilege of singing the same role with the Michigan Opera Company.

Several summers after the school year was over, Ed and I would go to Hamilton, Ontario, where in their Opera Festival Productions with the McMaster University's Orchestra, I sang a number of complete roles such as Santuzza in *Cavalleria Rusticana* by Pietro Mascagni; also to rave reviews, the lead in Georges Bizet's masterpiece *Carmen*.

Successful performances and reviews did not matter. I was discontented with my own voice and had lost the joy of singing. Finally I decided it was emotionally too costly to keep up with the struggle, and so this time I gave up singing for good. Giving up singing was as traumatic an experience as amputating your own limb, extremely painful and permanent. For a while I went through a mourning period for my loss. Yet at the end of devastating experiences, there must of necessity come a time of acceptance, and finally a healing.

Two years had gone by in which I had done no singing, not even in the shower, so naturally my voice had become totally lazy and completely rusty. However, even with those drawbacks, kicking, screaming, and after passionate arguments, still I was successfully drafted into the current Toledo Dinner Theater's production.

We performed seven shows a week for three whole months. During those productions I came to appreciate and welcome the challenges that a musical imposes on its performers, training them to becoming better actors.

Though I was not content with my own singing, yet my performances were well received and congratulated by audiences and the theater management alike. In fact, several years had passed when a couple of times, as a compliment, I was greeted as Mary by total strangers. I accepted their compliments with gratitude and mixed feelings.

So my very last public and professional engagement was the role of Bloody Mary in the musical *South Pacific*. A Broadway-type theatrical performance was a new experience for me; I treasured the beautiful work of Rodgers and Hammerstein and called it a genuine American operetta.

With that, my passion for singing and acting combined, I had a final hurray, graciously took my very last bow, and said a nostalgic, teary good-bye to the performing arts for good, the profession in which I had worked hard for many years.

I thank you, Lord, for past opportunities. You satisfy every need.

Chapter Twenty-Four

Passing the Torch

Before my commitment to the local dinner theater, I had already accepted a teaching position for individual piano and voice lessons in a private finishing school for boys and girls. This highly acclaimed school provided their students with advanced education and prepared them for any of the Ivy League universities of their choice. At one time or another I taught kids from kindergarten through their high school graduation. It was rewarding to have several talented students who demonstrated, as young as they were, a definite promise for their future successful, various musical pursuits.

One of my students, a champion in several sports in the state of Ohio, studied both voice and piano with me. I am always reminded of how much she appreciates me as her teacher, for she owes her solid foundation in musical understanding to my dedication as an instructor. Also proficient in violin and the double bass, after high school she went on to graduate from the Northwestern University. Later, she created an ensemble of singers and instrumentalists; to this day she writes some of their music and performs with them.

Another was a quiet and gentle boy who named me in the school's publication as one of the most influential teachers in his musical development. While he took piano lessons from me, simultaneously he continued and successfully matured in his viola performances as well. Today this young man is the founder and director of the Arneis Ensemble, a chamber music group dedicated to exploring interdisciplinary connections between music and other fields. Besides his teaching profession, I am delighted to know that he also plays in three different orchestras in the Boston area,

One piano student I had was a thirteen-year-old girl who desperately wanted to take voice lessons as well. Christina announced to me that she *knew* she was going to become a professional singer. I clearly saw her resolve and heard the certainty in her voice; as young as she was, she was convinced and believed without a doubt that she was meant to be a singer. No amount of counseling or warnings of no guarantees discouraged her. I recognized that same sense of knowledge in her.

It takes much more than an obviously beautiful voice to break into a serious singing career. Beyond a God-given pair of exceptional vocal cords, one needs to have a good vocal technique, stage presence, knowledge of several languages, etc. Only very few are fortunate enough eventually to make a comfortable living at it. None of my logical explanations and arguments dissuaded or weakened Christina's resolve.

I knew for sure that she was simply too young for serious training; her vocal cords were not developed yet, and I told her so. I procrastinated and tried to dissuade her as long as I could with no results. After a whole school year of unsuccessfully trying to have me start giving her voice lessons, I learned from her mother that she was looking for a voice teacher in the Yellow Pages; that seriously scared me.

I had no idea who she was going to end up with as a teacher. Many inexperienced vocal coaches have ruined young voices, robbing them out of a career even before the young student had a chance. I finally agreed to train her with one very important condition: she was to accept and follow my lead without questions asked.

Singing in front of others is much harder than playing a musical instrument. As a singer you are your instrument by the fact that you own your vocal cords; you are also the artist who performs on it. Therefore, even a slight constructive criticism can be taken personally and hurt.

Christina had no problem playing the piano in my presence, but during her first two voice lessons, the poor girl opened her mouth, but not a sound came out of her. She was so painfully shy. By the next two lessons, I finally heard a very tiny, yet delightfully sweet, childlike voice; she had a comfortable two-octave range plus a God-given, perfect, natural placement. The potential she possessed was quite obvious from the start.

I taught, coached, and prepared Christina musically, artistically, and in the foreign languages she needed for a classically trained professional. We continued working together beyond her high school and university years; today that young girl, with many scholarships and awards to her name, is a graduate fellow from the University of Michigan, with her master's degree in vocal performance. She has a vast repertoire of classical, operatic, Broadway musicals and Negro spirituals.

Christina worked long and hard with perseverance, focus, and passion; she apprenticed and paid her dues for a long time. Finally, after so many years of hard work, she was ready. It was only then that I began to guide and help launch her into the inevitable beginning of her career, which she well deserved. Our relationship by then was more than a teacher and a student; she had already become a surrogate daughter.

She auditioned and performed countless times and in different places; she got her training years behind her by singing not only in the United States but also Canada, as well as Europe, where she was invited several times by different companies and orchestras.

I, as Christina's personal manager, was always aware of all the compliments she received, not only because of her voice, singing and acting ability, but for her personality, sweet disposition, and work ethics. All of these experiences had prepared her for what turned out to be the highlight of her life as a young artist, that is when she was invited to sing in Russia.

Ed and I accompanied her and witnessed what turned out to be a great turning point and the launching of her career. Christina performed in St. Petersburg's famous Hermitage Museum, Moscow's Philharmonic Hall, and the renowned Tchaikovsky Auditorium, which is the equivalent of our Carnegie Hall in New York.

She sang all of these exceptionally successful performances with the Moscow Chamber Orchestra, under the direction of the highly esteemed conductor, Maestro Constantine Orbelian.

I am so delighted and proud of Christina's successes. She is now happily married to a baritone and is raising a beautiful little girl, living in Germany. For the last thirteen seasons she has been an honored leading soprano at the Aalto-Musiktheater in Essen. As a bonus, she also has the privilege of traveling and performing regularly in other countries in Europe.

Now, I finally understand the reason for my many years of struggles, sweat, and tears to learn the art of singing; I also know in my heart the raison d'être for my demanding and exhausting journey till ultimately

I made it into the field of opera. These efforts, well-spent, were simply planting of seedlings, so that Christina many years later could eventually reap the fruits of my labor for her own bright operatic career.

Thank you, Lord, for the opportunities to bless the lives of others.

Chapter Twenty-Five

Merciful Healings

s for me, a lifelong singing career was never in the cards. Finally, nearly thirty years into our marriage, during a routine sinus examination by an ear/nose/throat specialist, we found out not one, but two reasons for the constant discontentment and frustration I had with my own singing. His conclusive diagnosis was that I had a severe case of non-allergic rhinitis. This was the lesser of the two evils.

Though free of all allergies, the patient with this condition suffers all year with identical symptoms: tearing, plugged-up sinuses with constant post-nasal drip, which in turn irritate the throat and makes the victim highly vulnerable to regular throat infections. Hello there! The first light bulb came on.

Had this been the only problem, and been discovered way back when, I would have been spared all the agony and self-blame for the deficiency in my singing ability.

One allergy pill would have easily fixed my problem.

But a far more serious, most detrimental, and irreversible problem became clear when the compassionate doctor asked who had butchered my throat. That's when the second bulb came on.

It was only then that I relived in horror the nightmarish tonsillectomy I had undergone at sixteen. I was victimized, literally tortured during a roughly executed and unsuccessfully anesthetized removal of my infected tonsils. It was still excruciatingly painful to recollect each merciless surgical cut I received at both sides of my throat from the hands of the so-called doctor. He then roughly pulled out each inflamed tonsil from its embedded spot and cut it loose. Afterwards, with a long, hooklike needle, the doctor—I mean the butcher—sewed together the throat tissues he had just torn apart.

Being wide awake and having an un-anesthetized throat during the whole procedure, I was constantly aware, feeling each and every knife assault; it was as if I was observing his every move, but was unable to scream for pain. *This experience was worse than animal cruelty!*

Finally, with lightning speed, it all made perfect sense. The mystery was solved. Now at last I knew the reason for the vocal difficulties I had been having for decades. At last I stopped blaming myself for what I thought were my own vocal inadequacies. That awareness alone lifted the personal huge responsibility and the heavy burden, which I had been carrying for years, off my shoulders.

A singer needs more than a pair of healthy vocal cords to be able to sing well. In time surgically induced scar tissues, of which apparently I had plenty in my throat, do harden, causing the throat muscles to tighten and lose their flexibility, making it impossible for them to expand and lift when necessary. This is a deterrent, a disadvantage, and a serious handicap for a singer.

Even with that disturbing knowledge, today I feel a deep contentment that my rough, rocky journey was all for a worthwhile purpose. Professionally, it prepared me thoroughly in every way—musically, vocally, artistically, dramatically, emotionally—to help direct someone else realize their dream and reach the top of their own career in my stead.

On a personal level, after a long journey full of trials and ups and downs, no matter how long, no matter how hard the road, I had to get to the right place at the right time to meet Ed.

Finally, I was convinced singing was never meant to be my lifelong career and vocation; but from the very beginning, God in his wisdom had simply used all of it for me to find my true destiny and the total fulfillment of my life.

We were never promised a bed of roses in life, but have constant assurances in Christ's own words that he will be with us always; he never will leave or forsake us. Even through tough times come, with his love and compassion he will strengthen and sustain us.

Ed's mother sadly had passed away when he was only fourteen. Almost to the day, a year after we were married, we also lost his sweet, soft-spoken father, who had been ailing for a number of years. Father had raised his second and younger son single-handedly from his early teens on.

Three months later, barely recovered from our first family loss, my own loving father who was in good health, also passed away suddenly; he was only sixty-three. During our deep personal losses we supported, helped, and drew strength from each other in our healing process.

Through our married life I survived three bouts of cancer. All three were found in their very early stages, and each time I was blessed with quick recuperation with the minimum of radiation and no chemotherapy. During my first contact with the disease, I prayed for Ed more than for myself, he had lost his mother to the same dreadful disease, breast cancer; this would have been a severely painful déjà vu for my darling.

A couple of days after my mastectomy, as I was praying in my hospital bed, totally unprepared for an experience of rapture, I sensed the presence of the Lord extraordinarily real. A few seconds in his loving and healing presence was sufficient; even before I got the final and positive results from the doctors, I knew in my heart that the cancer was gone. That was more than twenty-five years ago. What a blessing! My case was as easy as having a simple operation and then coming home, with no aftereffects. God spared us both.

Though a perfect candidate for an open-heart surgery, Ed's doctor did not inspire much hope, yet wanted to give angioplasty a chance to remove the 99.9 percent block from an artery in Ed's heart. Since they had wheeled him to the surgery room, I had been all alone in the waiting room praying for him and his doctor. I was relieved when after a while I felt that familiar calm, peaceful feeling and had the assurance that Ed was going to be all right. Forty-five minutes into the procedure, the surgical nurse from the operating room came to tell me that they did not think they would be able to get rid of the obstruction which was hindering a normal blood flow to Ed's heart. I simply told her to go back and tell the doctor not to give up on him, since I knew in my heart that the impasse in Ed's artery would open. And it did!

According to the attending surgeon, miraculously Ed did not need an open-heart, bypass surgery; later he advised me to be forewarned that the blockage in the same artery would reappear in a year or two, and that he would see us again at that time. Incredibly, that artery remained open for the next sixteen years. That's when we went in again, this time for a couple of stents that saved his life anew without major surgery.

One thing I have learned: when God is at the helm of our lives, he guides us through life's stormy waters and brings us to a safe harbor of his choosing. All through the years our loving God has been merciful and has showered us with innumerable blessings, not because we deserved them, but because of his immeasurable, divine grace.

Father, we thank you for all your mercies and your ever-present healing power in our lives.

Chapter Twenty-Six

Retirement and After

Soon after we were engaged, kiddingly I asked Ed how soon before he planned to retire; I knew that he was aware how much I enjoyed having him around. Ed was not only fun to be with, but much more than that, he was like a clean, cool breeze that refreshed my lonely, cumbersome life. Simply, he was the source of my joy! What I got from him was this cute, logical, and indirect answer: "I think for practical reasons, I should not retire just yet." It was obvious; we needed to survive, and somebody had to work for our living.

I had discovered from early on that Ed had no desire or ambition to move from the classroom to school administration. He knew his calling was to be a classroom teacher, to have a direct influence on the kids under his care. His desire was to infect his students with his own love and passion for social studies, history, geography, and the political intricacies of the past and current events.

After thirty-nine years of teaching, Ed retired, to the deep disappointment of the school. Besides a surprise party at a colleague's home, the school where he had taught for the last thirty-six years honored Ed with an impressive midday farewell celebration.

At that luncheon in the school cafeteria, it was quite moving: even male teachers were in tears to see him go. They felt the school atmosphere would not be the same without him.

On that occasion school administration, faculty, office staff, and custodians were all invited; this was what Ed had wanted. Also, instead of a gift for his retirement, my kind and generous husband had asked that donations be sent to the local homeless, and battered women's organizations. He also requested contributions to the high school Parents Teachers Students Association, which in turn established a yearly scholarship for a deserving student in my beloved's name. I was glad they respected his requests.

The last thing Ed wished for was that the high school students' string quartet play classical music during the meal; the young musicians were happy to accommodate. Moreover, in his honor, some of the younger teachers, who just a few years earlier had been Ed's students, lovingly composed a humorous song depicting their memories of him through the years. This they performed with great enthusiasm, to the immense amusement of all present.

After lunch they presented him with a T-shirt with a group picture of his colleagues. They all had a photo of Ed's face cleverly superimposed on each character, inscribed with their true sentiments. It read: "You can never have enough Tutelians."

Then we were all invited to watch a few of his colleagues dig a deep hole in front of Ed's classroom window; there they planted a small, beautiful maple tree and named it "Ed's Tree." Seeing the depth and genuine adoration they all had for my husband, I confess I was profoundly moved, visibly proud, and deeply touched.

Through his many years of teaching my darling husband had been a recipient of numerous honors and service awards; he received a Certificate of Appreciation and a plaque that named him an Outstanding Educator. After retirement, he was also honored by being selected to the Hall of Fame in his school system.

Presently Ed is quite active with the retired teachers' organizations and socially keeps in touch with them regularly. His interest, enthusiasm, and readiness to participate in deep conversations about literature, art, politics, and world history are just as strong as ever.

Several years later, due to a declining arthritic condition, I too needed to resign, and retired for a less stressful life. At that specific gathering there were faculty, staff, administration, and some parents. To entertain them, I mentioned several amusing events, incidences that had happened between me and my students through the years; that brought on hearty laughter. Those funny memories will remain with me for all time.

With words of genuine praise and great appreciation, I was honored publicly for my thirty-five years of devoted service. That was quite touching indeed! The administration also presented me with a generous gift to an exclusive spa, where besides other treatments I was pampered like royalty with an hour of a magnificent therapeutic massage. Boy, what perfect timing that was for my aching bones! That simply was the perfect gift.

Today we are in our golden years. We still have not lost our joie de vivre and feel quite young at heart. Socially we are active with friends and family, never retreating from making new acquaintances. Our passion for the arts has not diminished, so whenever possible we regularly attend concerts, recitals, operas, theater, well-chosen movies, or new exhibits at the Toledo Museum, plus there are always art galleries and lectures to pursue.

We also continue, with great enthusiasm, our travels to new horizons. More so than flying to places far from our shores, we enjoy taking cruises where we unpack and relax for a week or so. Meeting new people, visiting new countries, and learning more about other cultures is almost a hobby with us.

I will be forever grateful that on several occasions we took my mother on trips with us; she was quite lonely after losing Dad. The highlight of all the travels she took with us was the boat cruise to the Eastern Mediterranean. Even as a child I remember she had always wanted to visit the Holy Land.

During that three-week excursion, beside numerous Middle Eastern countries, we also stopped at the Israeli Port of Haifa. On the same day we took a bus tour to Jerusalem, the Old City, visited the Church of the Holy Sepulcher, the Western Wall, Via Dolorosa, Bethlehem, and many other biblical touristic spots.

This was my mother's lifelong dream; she had never thought that some day it will come true. One of my greatest joys in life was to take her there; Ed and I made it possible for her to realize her greatest wish. We helped her dream come true as she had done for me so many years ago. "One good deed deserves another." Yes?

It was on that same cruise that Ed's great desire to visit Egypt came true as well; he had always wanted to see my birthplace. Besides, as a teacher of world history, he strongly believed that in addition to reading and studying about countries, the people, and their culture, it was important for him to visit those places personally to see and experience as many of them firsthand as possible.

For me going back to Egypt after twenty-two years was naturally nostalgic, a trip full of mixed sentiments. When visiting old landmarks and driving through familiar streets, it seemed I had only dreamt of those places before, like a transplanted tree coming back to rediscover the original soil from where it had its beginnings, roots, and nurturing. Through the years some things had changed, and yet, many had remained the same. It seems in the Middle East life changes much slower than in the West.

The one trip that perhaps was the most emotional for both Ed and me several years later was the guided tour to Armenia, the land of our forefathers. Armenia, an ancient country from biblical times, has survived throughout history; its ancient temples from the pre-Christian era still stand, to the amazement of tourists.

The first country to adopt Christianity as its official religion in 301 AD, the Armenian Church is the world's oldest national church. An earliest center of Christianity, the origin of the church is traced to the missions of the first century Apostles. Through the centuries the stone-built churches and monasteries are still preserved and found all over the country.

As far back as four or five generations, our ancestors, having lost their independence, were forced to move from their homeland. Many of them out of necessity migrated to faraway foreign lands, establishing themselves as families, churches, and communities. They built lucrative businesses for themselves and their children, only to migrate again and start the cycle all over again.

Armenians are literally dispersed throughout the world due to tragic historic circumstances. Amazingly most of them have become quite successful in whatever field they have pursued in life. Hence, I am the Egyptian, and Ed is the American born Armenian.

Throughout our married life, besides traveling within the United States and Canada, Ed and I have gone on trips and cruises that have taken us from Russia to the South Pacific and everything in between. Besides many of the Eastern Mediterranean countries, we also took a cruise to the Western Mediterranean, European ports, to the Caribbean, Bahamas, Central America, and crossed the Panama Canal cruising from San Diego to Fort Lauderdale. We have been and still are so very richly blessed, and do enjoy life to the fullest.

After forty-four years, we still have kept a healthy dose of humor alive in our marriage, remaining lovers and constant best friends to each other. We appreciate the preciousness and the brevity of life, remembering daily to count our blessings **with thanksgiving**; remaining faithful in every joyful or sorrowful experience, keeping in mind always that the love of God is the source of our abiding joy and successful marriage. Together we are still a work in progress. Our cup runs over (Psalm 23:5).

"For I know the plans I have for you, declares the Lord, plans to prosper you and not to harm you, plans to give you hope and a future" (Jeremiah 29:11).

Chapter Twenty-Seven

Final Thoughts

At the sunset of my life's journey, from time to time I look back with the sole purpose of thanksgiving. Going down memory lane fills me with awe even today as I retrace it in my mind and watch it like a movie; I view each episode of my story with great amazement, and marvel how, through many moons, I was led by God in each and every step. When things got tough, he without fail sent some of his many angels in human form into my life to help and to guide.

Going way back, I see myself through the years growing up and maturing from a very young, shy, and insecure child to a fairly self-confident and, according to some, rather a strong woman. At every corner and turn in my walk of life, I see God revisit me with his abundant, inexhaustible love and care; the one blessing that stands alone that I cherish the most is his greatest gift of all: the one and only love of my life.

Throughout the years both Ed and I have taken great pleasure in sharing our lives' experiences with others. We have found that sharing the lessons we have learned in the school of life, is a good way to bond with new friends.

In my communications with others, I have discovered that a number of people nostalgically dream of their past, often wishing for the good old days. All their efforts to conjure them up to relive those happier days gone by fail miserably and never seem to work. These groups of people live constantly with a sense of loss; they in vain try to restore their past. What a waste of time and energy!

Sadly, perhaps in actuality those times were not so wonderful after all: I believe that mercifully we somehow dilute from our memory the devastating effects of the difficulties we endured during those very same good old days.

Others, in the exact opposite way, even after fifty or sixty years of living, still see only the negative side of their lives; to this day they mourn over painful struggles, tragic experiences, and overwhelming failures they might have had to undergo in their past.

Listening to them carefully, you will see that they live continuously—perhaps will live the rest of their lives as well—frustrated with regrets for missed opportunities, wrong decisions, marriages gone sour, lost chances for wealth, and the fact that the career they always hoped for never materialized.

You find that at the top of their list, the reason for their deepest discontent is their realization that they cannot, or will never be able to, recover their losses. These dear souls live continuously under distress, uselessly carrying painful memories till the end of their lives; you will find them always unhappy and frustrated.

Both of these groups of people live with regrets; victims of their past, they have no vision for a fulfilling and a meaningful future. There is no joy left for the remaining few years of their lives.

In the sunset of life one can still maintain hope for a fruitful life and become a source of wisdom and blessing to the young. Among some people, a positive attitude, which is essential for well-being, often is nonexistent, or at best is in very short supply. Particularly for many seniors, life is already over before it is truly over. How sad.

"Where there is no vision, the people perish" (PROVERBS 29:18 KING JAMES VERSION).

But as for me, my purpose of revisiting or reliving the memories of the precious life God has granted me somehow differs from others'. I reminisce merely to rejoice. Gladly I share with others the miracles I still delight in and marvel at, as to how God in his mercy, grace, and love walked each step with me through my stressful and painful experiences. But most of all, it gives me joy to express my gratefulness for the One who brought me out of my troubles, and planted my feet on solid ground.

It is always in hindsight that we see God's blessings when the going was tough. Oh, that we could only walk by faith and not by sight (2ND CORINTHIANS 5:7).

Today the basic reason I am happy and content with my life is no big secret: even through trials I practice daily Ephesians 5:20, *"Giving* **thanks always for all things** *to God the Father"* (NKJV, EMPHASIS ADDED).

I know and understand perfectly well that it is not easy, neither it is normal, for any of us to always give thanks, particularly when things go desperately wrong. During failures and tragedies, especially when without warning sickness and sorrow hit us from left field, it feels unnatural to be thankful. But we are admonished: **"In everything** *by prayer and petition, with thanksgiving, present your requests to God"* (PHILIPPIANS 4:6 (NIV, EMPHASIS ADDED).

During difficult times, only by faith, not feeling, we know for sure that the Lord is infinitely closer, intensely real, and ever-present. He strengthens and consoles us as he walks along, and when we are not able to take another step, he gently carries us. That kind of faith is sufficient to build up our love and trust in him. I rejoice, for his promise still holds true even today: *"I am always with you, even unto the end of time"* (MATTHEW 28:20, PARAPHRASED AND EMPHASIS ADDED).

Interestingly, these two verses, Ephesians 5:20 and Matthew 28:20 seem to complement each other: *"Give thanks always, for I am always with you"* (PARAPHRASED, EMPHASIS ADDED).

I strongly believe that in genuine thanksgiving there is a deep and enduring contentment. Therein hides the source of the most precious gifts from above: faith, hope, love, peace, and abiding joy.

I also believe there is still time to grow deeper, change, and mature, even after seventy-five years of life. With God's grace the best is yet to come! Hallelujah!

Biography

Astrig Tutelian, a first time author, encouraged by those who knew a few bits and pieces of her life, motivated with a profound desire to encourage others to establish an unshakable trust in the faithfulness of God in every aspect of life, after many years of thoughtful considerations, casually started to put down her thoughts on paper which eventually gave birth to this book.

The author was born in Egypt into a devoted Armenian Christian family. This painfully shy, inexperienced and insecure child brought up quite conservatively, led by an inexplicable strong conviction that she should come to America, left home, family, church, community, and on her own, at nineteen, was on her way to the United States.

She recieved her formal musical education in California and Canada. After many struggles she became a professional singer, gave classical vocal concerts and for three seasons sang with the Metropolitan Opera Company. After marriage she devoted herself to a greatly satisfying teaching career.

Tributes:

"*My lessons with...Astrig Tutelian on piano was very formative in my musical growth.*" -Daniel Dona

Daniel is the founder, director and performer with the Arneis Ensemble, also performs with several orchestras in the east coast.

"*I met Astrig Tutelian at Maumee Valley Country Day School and without her, I doubt I would have gone on to study classical music. She continues to be a very good friend and mentor for me...without her friendship and guidance, I would not still be working as an opera singer.*" -Christina Clark.

Christina is a leading soprano singing continually to rave reviews. She has been for the past fourteen years with the Essen Opera Theater, in Germany.